ASTB-E

SECRETS

Study Guide
Your Key to Exam Success

Math 30 q 25 m SO s/q

DEAR FUTURE EXAM SUCCESS STORY

First of all, **THANK YOU** for purchasing Mometrix study materials!

Second, congratulations! You are one of the few determined test-takers who are committed to doing whatever it takes to excel on your exam. **You have come to the right place.** We developed these study materials with one goal in mind: to deliver you the information you need in a format that's concise and easy to use.

In addition to optimizing your guide for the content of the test, we've outlined our recommended steps for breaking down the preparation process into small, attainable goals so you can make sure you stay on track.

We've also analyzed the entire test-taking process, identifying the most common pitfalls and showing how you can overcome them and be ready for any curveball the test throws you.

Standardized testing is one of the biggest obstacles on your road to success, which only increases the importance of doing well in the high-pressure, high-stakes environment of test day. Your results on this test could have a significant impact on your future, and this guide provides the information and practical advice to help you achieve your full potential on test day.

Your success is our success

We would love to hear from you! If you would like to share the story of your exam success or if you have any questions or comments in regard to our products, please contact us at **800-673-8175** or **support@mometrix.com**.

Thanks again for your business and we wish you continued success!

Sincerely,
The Mometrix Test Preparation Team

TABLE OF CONTENTS

Introduction

Thank you for purchasing this resource! You have made the choice to prepare yourself for a test that could have a huge impact on your future, and this guide is designed to help you be fully ready for test day. Obviously, it's important to have a solid understanding of the test material, but you also need to be prepared for the unique environment and stressors of the test, so that you can perform to the best of your abilities.

For this purpose, the first section that appears in this guide is the **Secret Keys**. We've devoted countless hours to meticulously researching what works and what doesn't, and we've boiled down our findings to the five most impactful steps you can take to improve your performance on the test. We start at the beginning with study planning and move through the preparation process, all the way to the testing strategies that will help you get the most out of what you know when you're finally sitting in front of the test.

We recommend that you start preparing for your test as far in advance as possible. However, if you've bought this guide as a last-minute study resource and only have a few days before your test, we recommend that you skip over the first two Secret Keys since they address a long-term study plan.

If you struggle with **test anxiety**, we strongly encourage you to check out our recommendations for how you can overcome it. Test anxiety is a formidable foe, but it can be beaten, and we want to make sure you have the tools you need to defeat it.

Secret Key #1 – Plan Big, Study Small

There's a lot riding on your performance. If you want to ace this test, you're going to need to keep your skills sharp and the material fresh in your mind. You need a plan that lets you review everything you need to know while still fitting in your schedule. We'll break this strategy down into three categories.

Information Organization

Start with the information you already have: the official test outline. From this, you can make a complete list of all the concepts you need to cover before the test. Organize these concepts into groups that can be studied together, and create a list of any related vocabulary you need to learn so you can brush up on any difficult terms. You'll want to keep this vocabulary list handy once you actually start studying since you may need to add to it along the way.

Time Management

Once you have your set of study concepts, decide how to spread them out over the time you have left before the test. Break your study plan into small, clear goals so you have a manageable task for each day and know exactly what you're doing. Then just focus on one small step at a time. When you manage your time this way, you don't need to spend hours at a time studying. Studying a small block of content for a short period each day helps you retain information better and avoid stressing over how much you have left to do. You can relax knowing that you have a plan to cover everything in time. In order for this strategy to be effective though, you have to start studying early and stick to your schedule. Avoid the exhaustion and futility that comes from last-minute cramming!

Study Environment

The environment you study in has a big impact on your learning. Studying in a coffee shop, while probably more enjoyable, is not likely to be as fruitful as studying in a quiet room. It's important to keep distractions to a minimum. You're only planning to study for a short block of time, so make the most of it. Don't pause to check your phone or get up to find a snack. It's also important to **avoid multitasking**. Research has consistently shown that multitasking will make your studying dramatically less effective. Your study area should also be comfortable and well-lit so you don't have the distraction of straining your eyes or sitting on an uncomfortable chair.

The time of day you study is also important. You want to be rested and alert. Don't wait until just before bedtime. Study when you'll be most likely to comprehend and remember. Even better, if you know what time of day your test will be, set that time aside for study. That way your brain will be used to working on that subject at that specific time and you'll have a better chance of recalling information.

Finally, it can be helpful to team up with others who are studying for the same test. Your actual studying should be done in as isolated an environment as possible, but the work of organizing the information and setting up the study plan can be divided up. In between study sessions, you can discuss with your teammates the concepts that you're all studying and quiz each other on the details. Just be sure that your teammates are as serious about the test as you are. If you find that your study time is being replaced with social time, you might need to find a new team.

Secret Key #2 – Make Your Studying Count

You're devoting a lot of time and effort to preparing for this test, so you want to be absolutely certain it will pay off. This means doing more than just reading the content and hoping you can remember it on test day. It's important to make every minute of study count. There are two main areas you can focus on to make your studying count:

Retention

It doesn't matter how much time you study if you can't remember the material. You need to make sure you are retaining the concepts. To check your retention of the information you're learning, try recalling it at later times with minimal prompting. Try carrying around flashcards and glance at one or two from time to time or ask a friend who's also studying for the test to quiz you.

To enhance your retention, look for ways to put the information into practice so that you can apply it rather than simply recalling it. If you're using the information in practical ways, it will be much easier to remember. Similarly, it helps to solidify a concept in your mind if you're not only reading it to yourself but also explaining it to someone else. Ask a friend to let you teach them about a concept you're a little shaky on (or speak aloud to an imaginary audience if necessary). As you try to summarize, define, give examples, and answer your friend's questions, you'll understand the concepts better and they will stay with you longer. Finally, step back for a big picture view and ask yourself how each piece of information fits with the whole subject. When you link the different concepts together and see them working together as a whole, it's easier to remember the individual components.

Finally, practice showing your work on any multi-step problems, even if you're just studying. Writing out each step you take to solve a problem will help solidify the process in your mind, and you'll be more likely to remember it during the test.

Modality

Modality simply refers to the means or method by which you study. Choosing a study modality that fits your own individual learning style is crucial. No two people learn best in exactly the same way, so it's important to know your strengths and use them to your advantage.

For example, if you learn best by visualization, focus on visualizing a concept in your mind and draw an image or a diagram. Try color-coding your notes, illustrating them, or creating symbols that will trigger your mind to recall a learned concept. If you learn best by hearing or discussing information, find a study partner who learns the same way or read aloud to yourself. Think about how to put the information in your own words. Imagine that you are giving a lecture on the topic and record yourself so you can listen to it later.

For any learning style, flashcards can be helpful. Organize the information so you can take advantage of spare moments to review. Underline key words or phrases. Use different colors for different categories. Mnemonic devices (such as creating a short list in which every item starts with the same letter) can also help with retention. Find what works best for you and use it to store the information in your mind most effectively and easily.

Secret Key #3 – Practice the Right Way

Your success on test day depends not only on how many hours you put into preparing, but also on whether you prepared the right way. It's good to check along the way to see if your studying is paying off. One of the most effective ways to do this is by taking practice tests to evaluate your progress. Practice tests are useful because they show exactly where you need to improve. Every time you take a practice test, pay special attention to these three groups of questions:

- The questions you got wrong
- The questions you had to guess on, even if you guessed right
- The questions you found difficult or slow to work through

This will show you exactly what your weak areas are, and where you need to devote more study time. Ask yourself why each of these questions gave you trouble. Was it because you didn't understand the material? Was it because you didn't remember the vocabulary? Do you need more repetitions on this type of question to build speed and confidence? Dig into those questions and figure out how you can strengthen your weak areas as you go back to review the material.

Additionally, many practice tests have a section explaining the answer choices. It can be tempting to read the explanation and think that you now have a good understanding of the concept. However, an explanation likely only covers part of the question's broader context. Even if the explanation makes sense, **go back and investigate** every concept related to the question until you're positive you have a thorough understanding.

As you go along, keep in mind that the practice test is just that: practice. Memorizing these questions and answers will not be very helpful on the actual test because it is unlikely to have any of the same exact questions. If you only know the right answers to the sample questions, you won't be prepared for the real thing. **Study the concepts** until you understand them fully, and then you'll be able to answer any question that shows up on the test.

It's important to wait on the practice tests until you're ready. If you take a test on your first day of study, you may be overwhelmed by the amount of material covered and how much you need to learn. Work up to it gradually.

On test day, you'll need to be prepared for answering questions, managing your time, and using the test-taking strategies you've learned. It's a lot to balance, like a mental marathon that will have a big impact on your future. Like training for a marathon, you'll need to start slowly and work your way up. When test day arrives, you'll be ready.

Start with the strategies you've read in the first two Secret Keys—plan your course and study in the way that works best for you. If you have time, consider using multiple study resources to get different approaches to the same concepts. It can be helpful to see difficult concepts from more than one angle. Then find a good source for practice tests. Many times, the test website will suggest potential study resources or provide sample tests.

Practice Test Strategy

If you're able to find at least three practice tests, we recommend this strategy:

UNTIMED AND OPEN-BOOK PRACTICE

Take the first test with no time constraints and with your notes and study guide handy. Take your time and focus on applying the strategies you've learned.

TIMED AND OPEN-BOOK PRACTICE

Take the second practice test open-book as well, but set a timer and practice pacing yourself to finish in time.

TIMED AND CLOSED-BOOK PRACTICE

Take any other practice tests as if it were test day. Set a timer and put away your study materials. Sit at a table or desk in a quiet room, imagine yourself at the testing center, and answer questions as quickly and accurately as possible.

Keep repeating timed and closed-book tests on a regular basis until you run out of practice tests or it's time for the actual test. Your mind will be ready for the schedule and stress of test day, and you'll be able to focus on recalling the material you've learned.

Secret Key #4 – Pace Yourself

Once you're fully prepared for the material on the test, your biggest challenge on test day will be managing your time. Just knowing that the clock is ticking can make you panic even if you have plenty of time left. Work on pacing yourself so you can build confidence against the time constraints of the exam. Pacing is a difficult skill to master, especially in a high-pressure environment, so **practice is vital**.

Set time expectations for your pace based on how much time is available. For example, if a section has 60 questions and the time limit is 30 minutes, you know you have to average 30 seconds or less per question in order to answer them all. Although 30 seconds is the hard limit, set 25 seconds per question as your goal, so you reserve extra time to spend on harder questions. When you budget extra time for the harder questions, you no longer have any reason to stress when those questions take longer to answer.

Don't let this time expectation distract you from working through the test at a calm, steady pace, but keep it in mind so you don't spend too much time on any one question. Recognize that taking extra time on one question you don't understand may keep you from answering two that you do understand later in the test. If your time limit for a question is up and you're still not sure of the answer, mark it and move on, and come back to it later if the time and the test format allow. If the testing format doesn't allow you to return to earlier questions, just make an educated guess; then put it out of your mind and move on.

On the easier questions, be careful not to rush. It may seem wise to hurry through them so you have more time for the challenging ones, but it's not worth missing one if you know the concept and just didn't take the time to read the question fully. Work efficiently but make sure you understand the question and have looked at all of the answer choices, since more than one may seem right at first.

Even if you're paying attention to the time, you may find yourself a little behind at some point. You should speed up to get back on track, but do so wisely. Don't panic; just take a few seconds less on each question until you're caught up. Don't guess without thinking, but do look through the answer choices and eliminate any you know are wrong. If you can get down to two choices, it is often worthwhile to guess from those. Once you've chosen an answer, move on and don't dwell on any that you skipped or had to hurry through. If a question was taking too long, chances are it was one of the harder ones, so you weren't as likely to get it right anyway.

On the other hand, if you find yourself getting ahead of schedule, it may be beneficial to slow down a little. The more quickly you work, the more likely you are to make a careless mistake that will affect your score. You've budgeted time for each question, so don't be afraid to spend that time. Practice an efficient but careful pace to get the most out of the time you have.

6

Secret Key #5 – Have a Plan for Guessing

When you're taking the test, you may find yourself stuck on a question. Some of the answer choices seem better than others, but you don't see the one answer choice that is obviously correct. What do you do?

The scenario described above is very common, yet most test takers have not effectively prepared for it. Developing and practicing a plan for guessing may be one of the single most effective uses of your time as you get ready for the exam.

In developing your plan for guessing, there are three questions to address:

- When should you start the guessing process?
- How should you narrow down the choices?
- Which answer should you choose?

When to Start the Guessing Process

Unless your plan for guessing is to select C every time (which, despite its merits, is not what we recommend), you need to leave yourself enough time to apply your answer elimination strategies. Since you have a limited amount of time for each question, that means that if you're going to give yourself the best shot at guessing correctly, you have to decide quickly whether or not you will guess.

Of course, the best-case scenario is that you don't have to guess at all, so first, see if you can answer the question based on your knowledge of the subject and basic reasoning skills. Focus on the key words in the question and try to jog your memory of related topics. Give yourself a chance to bring the knowledge to mind, but once you realize that you don't have (or you can't access) the knowledge you need to answer the question, it's time to start the guessing process.

It's almost always better to start the guessing process too early than too late. It only takes a few seconds to remember something and answer the question from knowledge. Carefully eliminating wrong answer choices takes longer. Plus, going through the process of eliminating answer choices can actually help jog your memory.

Summary: Start the guessing process as soon as you decide that you can't answer the question based on your knowledge.

How to Narrow Down the Choices

The next chapter in this book (**Test-Taking Strategies**) includes a wide range of strategies for how to approach questions and how to look for answer choices to eliminate. You will definitely want to read those carefully, practice them, and figure out which ones work best for you. Here though, we're going to address a mindset rather than a particular strategy.

Your chances of guessing an answer correctly depend on how many options you are choosing from.

How many choices you have	How likely you are to guess correctly
5	20%
4	25%
3	33%
2	50%
1	100%

You can see from this chart just how valuable it is to be able to eliminate incorrect answers and make an educated guess, but there are two things that many test takers do that cause them to miss out on the benefits of guessing:

- Accidentally eliminating the correct answer
- Selecting an answer based on an impression

We'll look at the first one here, and the second one in the next section.

To avoid accidentally eliminating the correct answer, we recommend a thought exercise called **the $5 challenge**. In this challenge, you only eliminate an answer choice from contention if you are willing to bet $5 on it being wrong. Why $5? Five dollars is a small but not insignificant amount of money. It's an amount you could afford to lose but wouldn't want to throw away. And while losing $5 once might not hurt too much, doing it twenty times will set you back $100. In the same way, each small decision you make—eliminating a choice here, guessing on a question there—won't by itself impact your score very much, but when you put them all together, they can make a big difference. By holding each answer choice elimination decision to a higher standard, you can reduce the risk of accidentally eliminating the correct answer.

The $5 challenge can also be applied in a positive sense: If you are willing to bet $5 that an answer choice *is* correct, go ahead and mark it as correct.

Summary: Only eliminate an answer choice if you are willing to bet $5 that it is wrong.

Which Answer to Choose

You're taking the test. You've run into a hard question and decided you'll have to guess. You've eliminated all the answer choices you're willing to bet $5 on. Now you have to pick an answer. Why do we even need to talk about this? Why can't you just pick whichever one you feel like when the time comes?

The answer to these questions is that if you don't come into the test with a plan, you'll rely on your impression to select an answer choice, and if you do that, you risk falling into a trap. The test writers know that everyone who takes their test will be guessing on some of the questions, so they intentionally write wrong answer choices to seem plausible. You still have to pick an answer though, and if the wrong answer choices are designed to look right, how can you ever be sure that you're not falling for their trap? The best solution we've found to this dilemma is to take the decision out of your hands entirely. Here is the process we recommend:

Once you've eliminated any choices that you are confident (willing to bet $5) are wrong, select the first remaining choice as your answer.

Whether you choose to select the first remaining choice, the second, or the last, the important thing is that you use some preselected standard. Using this approach guarantees that you will not be enticed into selecting an answer choice that looks right, because you are not basing your decision on how the answer choices look.

This is not meant to make you question your knowledge. Instead, it is to help you recognize the difference between your knowledge and your impressions. There's a huge difference between thinking an answer is right because of what you know, and thinking an answer is right because it looks or sounds like it should be right.

Summary: To ensure that your selection is appropriately random, make a predetermined selection from among all answer choices you have not eliminated.

Test-Taking Strategies

This section contains a list of test-taking strategies that you may find helpful as you work through the test. By taking what you know and applying logical thought, you can maximize your chances of answering any question correctly!

It is very important to realize that every question is different and every person is different: no single strategy will work on every question, and no single strategy will work for every person. That's why we've included all of them here, so you can try them out and determine which ones work best for different types of questions and which ones work best for you.

Question Strategies

READ CAREFULLY

Read the question and answer choices carefully. Don't miss the question because you misread the terms. You have plenty of time to read each question thoroughly and make sure you understand what is being asked. Yet a happy medium must be attained, so don't waste too much time. You must read carefully, but efficiently.

CONTEXTUAL CLUES

Look for contextual clues. If the question includes a word you are not familiar with, look at the immediate context for some indication of what the word might mean. Contextual clues can often give you all the information you need to decipher the meaning of an unfamiliar word. Even if you can't determine the meaning, you may be able to narrow down the possibilities enough to make a solid guess at the answer to the question.

PREFIXES

If you're having trouble with a word in the question or answer choices, try dissecting it. Take advantage of every clue that the word might include. Prefixes and suffixes can be a huge help. Usually they allow you to determine a basic meaning. Pre- means before, post- means after, pro - is positive, de- is negative. From prefixes and suffixes, you can get an idea of the general meaning of the word and try to put it into context.

HEDGE WORDS

Watch out for critical hedge words, such as *likely*, *may*, *can*, *sometimes*, *often*, *almost*, *mostly*, *usually*, *generally*, *rarely*, and *sometimes*. Question writers insert these hedge phrases to cover every possibility. Often an answer choice will be wrong simply because it leaves no room for exception. Be on guard for answer choices that have definitive words such as *exactly* and *always*.

SWITCHBACK WORDS

Stay alert for *switchbacks*. These are the words and phrases frequently used to alert you to shifts in thought. The most common switchback words are *but*, *although*, and *however*. Others include *nevertheless*, *on the other hand*, *even though*, *while*, *in spite of*, *despite*, *regardless of*. Switchback words are important to catch because they can change the direction of the question or an answer choice.

FACE VALUE

When in doubt, use common sense. Accept the situation in the problem at face value. Don't read too much into it. These problems will not require you to make wild assumptions. If you have to go beyond creativity and warp time or space in order to have an answer choice fit the question, then you should move on and

10

consider the other answer choices. These are normal problems rooted in reality. The applicable relationship or explanation may not be readily apparent, but it is there for you to figure out. Use your common sense to interpret anything that isn't clear.

Answer Choice Strategies

ANSWER SELECTION

The most thorough way to pick an answer choice is to identify and eliminate wrong answers until only one is left, then confirm it is the correct answer. Sometimes an answer choice may immediately seem right, but be careful. The test writers will usually put more than one reasonable answer choice on each question, so take a second to read all of them and make sure that the other choices are not equally obvious. As long as you have time left, it is better to read every answer choice than to pick the first one that looks right without checking the others.

ANSWER CHOICE FAMILIES

An answer choice family consists of two (in rare cases, three) answer choices that are very similar in construction and cannot all be true at the same time. If you see two answer choices that are direct opposites or parallels, one of them is usually the correct answer. For instance, if one answer choice says that quantity x increases and another either says that quantity x decreases (opposite) or says that quantity y increases (parallel), then those answer choices would fall into the same family. An answer choice that doesn't match the construction of the answer choice family is more likely to be incorrect. Most questions will not have answer choice families, but when they do appear, you should be prepared to recognize them.

ELIMINATE ANSWERS

Eliminate answer choices as soon as you realize they are wrong, but make sure you consider all possibilities. If you are eliminating answer choices and realize that the last one you are left with is also wrong, don't panic. Start over and consider each choice again. There may be something you missed the first time that you will realize on the second pass.

AVOID FACT TRAPS

Don't be distracted by an answer choice that is factually true but doesn't answer the question. You are looking for the choice that answers the question. Stay focused on what the question is asking for so you don't accidentally pick an answer that is true but incorrect. Always go back to the question and make sure the answer choice you've selected actually answers the question and is not merely a true statement.

EXTREME STATEMENTS

In general, you should avoid answers that put forth extreme actions as standard practice or proclaim controversial ideas as established fact. An answer choice that states the "process should be used in certain situations, if..." is much more likely to be correct than one that states the "process should be discontinued completely." The first is a calm rational statement and doesn't even make a definitive, uncompromising stance, using a hedge word *if* to provide wiggle room, whereas the second choice is a radical idea and far more extreme.

BENCHMARK

As you read through the answer choices and you come across one that seems to answer the question well, mentally select that answer choice. This is not your final answer, but it's the one that will help you evaluate the other answer choices. The one that you selected is your benchmark or standard for judging each of the other answer choices. Every other answer choice must be compared to your benchmark. That

Copyright © Mometrix Media. You have been licensed one copy of this document for personal use only. Any other reproduction or redistribution is strictly prohibited. All rights reserved.

choice is correct until proven otherwise by another answer choice beating it. If you find a better answer, then that one becomes your new benchmark. Once you've decided that no other choice answers the question as well as your benchmark, you have your final answer.

PREDICT THE ANSWER

Before you even start looking at the answer choices, it is often best to try to predict the answer. When you come up with the answer on your own, it is easier to avoid distractions and traps because you will know exactly what to look for. The right answer choice is unlikely to be word-for-word what you came up with, but it should be a close match. Even if you are confident that you have the right answer, you should still take the time to read each option before moving on.

General Strategies

TOUGH QUESTIONS

If you are stumped on a problem or it appears too hard or too difficult, don't waste time. Move on! Remember though, if you can quickly check for obviously incorrect answer choices, your chances of guessing correctly are greatly improved. Before you completely give up, at least try to knock out a couple of possible answers. Eliminate what you can and then guess at the remaining answer choices before moving on.

CHECK YOUR WORK

Since you will probably not know every term listed and the answer to every question, it is important that you get credit for the ones that you do know. Don't miss any questions through careless mistakes. If at all possible, try to take a second to look back over your answer selection and make sure you've selected the correct answer choice and haven't made a costly careless mistake (such as marking an answer choice that you didn't mean to mark). This quick double check should more than pay for itself in caught mistakes for the time it costs.

PACE YOURSELF

It's easy to be overwhelmed when you're looking at a page full of questions; your mind is confused and full of random thoughts, and the clock is ticking down faster than you would like. Calm down and maintain the pace that you have set for yourself. Especially as you get down to the last few minutes of the test, don't let the small numbers on the clock make you panic. As long as you are on track by monitoring your pace, you are guaranteed to have time for each question.

DON'T RUSH

It is very easy to make errors when you are in a hurry. Maintaining a fast pace in answering questions is pointless if it makes you miss questions that you would have gotten right otherwise. Test writers like to include distracting information and wrong answers that seem right. Taking a little extra time to avoid careless mistakes can make all the difference in your test score. Find a pace that allows you to be confident in the answers that you select.

KEEP MOVING

Panicking will not help you pass the test, so do your best to stay calm and keep moving. Taking deep breaths and going through the answer elimination steps you practiced can help to break through a stress barrier and keep your pace.

Final Notes

The combination of a solid foundation of content knowledge and the confidence that comes from practicing your plan for applying that knowledge is the key to maximizing your performance on test day. As your foundation of content knowledge is built up and strengthened, you'll find that the strategies included in this chapter become more and more effective in helping you quickly sift through the distractions and traps of the test to isolate the correct answer.

Now it's time to move on to the test content chapters of this book, but be sure to keep your goal in mind. As you read, think about how you will be able to apply this information on the test. If you've already seen sample questions for the test and you have an idea of the question format and style, try to come up with questions of your own that you can answer based on what you're reading. This will give you valuable practice applying your knowledge in the same ways you can expect to on test day.

Good luck and good studying!

ASTB-E Overview

The goal of becoming a military aviator is a noble one, and those who achieve it will have earned membership in a very elite class. Many people would like to become aviators, but few are up to the myriad demands and challenges that must be successfully met in order to reach their dream. It is a long and arduous journey, and it begins with performing well on a difficult aptitude test, above and beyond any other requirements for college degrees or percentile rank on broader military aptitude exams. These exams are known as aptitude tests, because they focus less on the knowledge a person already has and more on that person's ability to innately handle certain types of tasks.

There are two primary reasons the military requires aspiring aviators to pass these challenging exams. The first reason hinges on supply and demand. Simply put, the number of men and women interested in becoming aviators in the military is far higher than the number of pilots the various branches of the military actually need. The second primary factor is the enormous cost of training a military pilot. It has long been common knowledge that it costs well over a $1 million to train a pilot, but that now appears to be an outdated figure. It was recently reported that the Air Force spends approximately $6 million to train one fighter pilot. No matter what the exact figure is, training military pilots is extremely expensive. Before they commit to training a pilot, the military branches want to be pretty certain that he or she is up to the challenge, and won't wash out before completing training. These tests have been designed to select the candidates who are most likely to be excellent candidates for pilot training, and they have a long track record of being very accurate.

In the Navy, Marine Corps, and Coast Guard, the aptitude test used for selection into the flight training programs is the ASTB, which stands for Aviation Selection Test Battery. The current version of the test is known as the ASTB-E. Although the ASTB-E is considered to be an aptitude test, it is also a test of acquired knowledge and skills in some areas, such as aviation knowledge and math. The ASTB-E is a battery of seven different exams, or subtests. Three of the seven subtests form the OAR, or Officer Aptitude Rating. These subtests are Math Skills, Reading Comprehension, and Mechanical Comprehension. If for some reason, you're taking the ASTB-E for entrance into a non-aviation officer program, you may opt to complete only these three subtests.

The other four subtests, which together with the OAR subtests form the full ASTB-E, are the Aviation and Nautical Information Test, the Naval Aviation Trait Facet Inventory, the Performance Based Measures Battery, and the Biographical Inventory with Response Validation. Of these last four subtests, only the Aviation and Nautical Information Test can be academically prepared for. The Trait Facet Inventory and the Biographical Inventory are tests designed to evaluate your personality and background for traits common to successful pilots. Either you have these or you don't, and trying to trick the test is unwise. The tests are set up to sniff out any inconsistencies in your answers, so odds are they will be able to tell if you're bending the truth.

You can certainly do things to prepare for the Performance Based Measures Battery, but it will not be studying from a book. This section is a series of physical and mental tests designed to measure your mental processing speed, physical dexterity, and multi-tasking ability. While other military flight tests use multiple choice questions to test your spatial orientation abilities, the ASTB-E requires you to use simulated flight controls to effectively address situations involving the need for spatial orientation. We've included some spatial orientation questions at the back of the book in case you'd find it helpful to test your abilities using them, but the most helpful preparation for this set of tasks may be spending some time with flight simulation games, especially those that allow you to use controllers that resemble real flight controls.

The next few sections will go over in detail the subtests for which you can academically prepare to get you ready for what you will see on each test.

Math Skills Test

On this section of the ASTB-E, you'll be tested for your knowledge, skill, and aptitude in math. Being highly skilled at math is very important for anyone seeking to become a pilot, for many reasons. In order to make it successfully through aviator training, and then to succeed as a pilot, a person will need to be able to solve basic math problems rapidly, and in their head, without having time to work them out on a calculator or with a pencil and paper. Beyond this, however, the highly developed analytical skills that enable a person to quickly solve math problems will be useful in all sorts of different ways and in all kinds of different situations. So, while this section of the ASTB-E does test knowledge and abilities, it's also testing for general learning aptitude.

To do well on this section, you'll need to have a solid mastery of some of the math subjects taught through all four years of high school, and some lower level college courses. This subtest lasts 40 minutes, and you are not allowed to use a calculator. It's very important to keep in mind that the MST section is adaptive, and factor this into your approach.

The math section will begin with a question of medium difficulty. If you answer it correctly, you will then be given a harder question. If you answer that question correctly, the next question will be even more difficult. This process will continue until you get an answer wrong, at which point you will be given an easier question. Answer it right, and the questions will start getting harder again, but if you answer it wrong, the computer will keep giving you easier questions until you get one right.

If you answer the first question incorrectly, the process works in reverse, giving you an easier question right off the bat. The computer will adapt to a test taker's answers in this manner after every question, so the next question that will be displayed is not determined until after an answer has been submitted for the previous question.

Because of this, it's important to take the time to do your best on every question. Don't skip a question just because it seems hard. If you're answering questions right, the questions are supposed to get harder. At the same time though, you want to make sure you answer enough questions so that the computer can accurately identify your skill level. Not answering enough questions can hurt you even more than answering some questions incorrectly. As with everything, there is a balance to be struck, but with computer adaptive testing, that balance leans more heavily toward answering correctly than answering as many questions as possible.

The following sections outline the basic math concepts needed to excel on the Math Skills subtest. As someone who is interested in flight training, you've probably taken a lot of math tests in your educational career, but just in case, here is one of the most important things to remember as you study math concepts:

More so than in almost any other subject, **practice matters**. Math concepts are explained in ways that make you think you understand them well, but until you can quickly work practice problems several days after you read about the underlying concepts without referring back to them, you haven't actually internalized them.

Numbers and Their Classifications

Numbers are the basic building blocks of mathematics. Specific features of numbers are identified by the following terms:

- Integers – The set of whole positive and negative numbers, including zero. Integers do not include fractions $\left(\frac{1}{3}\right)$, decimals (0.56), or mixed numbers $\left(7\frac{3}{4}\right)$.
- Prime number – A whole number greater than 1 that has only two factors, itself and 1; that is, a number that can be divided evenly only by 1 and itself.
- Composite number – A whole number greater than 1 that has more than two different factors; in other words, any whole number that is not a prime number. For example: The composite number 8 has the factors of 1, 2, 4, and 8.
- Even number – Any integer that can be divided by 2 without leaving a remainder. For example: 2, 4, 6, 8, and so on.
- Odd number – Any integer that cannot be divided evenly by 2. For example: 3, 5, 7, 9, and so on.
- Decimal number – a number that uses a decimal point to show the part of the number that is less than one. Example: 1.234.
- Decimal point – a symbol used to separate the ones place from the tenths place in decimals or dollars from cents in currency.
- Decimal place – the position of a number to the right of the decimal point. In the decimal 0.123, the 1 is in the first place to the right of the decimal point, indicating tenths; the 2 is in the second place, indicating hundredths; and the 3 is in the third place, indicating thousandths.

> **Review Video: Numbers and Their Classifications**
> Visit mometrix.com/academy and enter code: 461071

The decimal, or base 10, system is a number system that uses ten different digits (0, 1, 2, 3, 4, 5, 6, 7, 8, 9). An example of a number system that uses something other than ten digits is the binary, or base 2, number system, used by computers, which uses only the numbers 0 and 1. It is thought that the decimal system originated because people had only their 10 fingers for counting.

Rational, irrational, and real numbers can be described as follows:

- Rational numbers include all integers, decimals, and fractions. Any terminating or repeating decimal number is a rational number.
- Irrational numbers cannot be written as fractions or decimals because the number of decimal places is infinite and there is no recurring pattern of digits within the number. For example, pi (π) begins with 3.141592 and continues without terminating or repeating, so pi is an irrational number.
- Real numbers are the set of all rational and irrational numbers.

Operations

There are four basic mathematical operations:

1. Addition increases the value of one quantity by the value of another quantity. *Example*: $2 + 4 = 6$; $8 + 9 = 17$. The result is called the sum. With addition, the order does not matter. $4 + 2 = 2 + 4$.

2. Subtraction is the opposite operation to addition; it decreases the value of one quantity by the value of another quantity. *Example*: $6 - 4 = 2$; $17 - 8 = 9$. The result is called the difference. Note that with subtraction, the order does matter. $6 - 4 \neq 4 - 6$.
3. Multiplication can be thought of as repeated addition. One number tells how many times to add the other number to itself. *Example*: 3×2 (three times two) $= 2 + 2 + 2 = 6$. With multiplication, the order does not matter. $2 \times 3 = 3 \times 2$ or $3 + 3 = 2 + 2 + 2$.
4. Division is the opposite operation to multiplication; one number tells us how many parts to divide the other number into. *Example*: $20 \div 4 = 5$; if 20 is split into 4 equal parts, each part is 5. With division, the order of the numbers does matter. $20 \div 4 \neq 4 \div 20$.

An exponent is a superscript number placed next to another number at the top right. It indicates how many times the base number is to be multiplied by itself. Exponents provide a shorthand way to write what would be a longer mathematical expression. *Example*: $a^2 = a \times a$; $2^4 = 2 \times 2 \times 2 \times 2$. A number with an exponent of 2 is said to be "squared," while a number with an exponent of 3 is said to be "cubed."

The value of a number raised to an exponent is called its power. So, 8^4 is read as "8 to the 4th power," or "8 raised to the power of 4." A negative exponent is the same as the reciprocal of a positive exponent. *Example*: $a^{-2} = \frac{1}{a^2}$.

Review Video: Exponents
Visit mometrix.com/academy and enter code: 600998

Parentheses are used to designate which operations should be done first when there are multiple operations. *Example*: $4 - (2 + 1) = 1$; the parentheses tell us that we must add 2 and 1, and then subtract the sum from 4, rather than subtracting 2 from 4 and then adding 1 (this would give us an answer of 3).

Order of Operations is a set of rules that dictates the order in which we must perform each operation in an expression so that we will evaluate it accurately. If we have an expression that includes multiple different operations, Order of Operations tells us which operations to do first. The most common mnemonic for Order of Operations is PEMDAS, or "Please Excuse My Dear Aunt Sally." PEMDAS stands for Parentheses, Exponents, Multiplication, Division, Addition, Subtraction. It is important to understand that multiplication and division have equal precedence, as do addition and subtraction, so those pairs of operations are simply worked from left to right in order.

Review Video: Order of Operations
Visit mometrix.com/academy and enter code: 259675

Example: Evaluate the expression $5 + 20 \div 4 \times (2 + 3)^2 - 6$ using the correct order of operations.

P: Perform the operations inside the parentheses, $(2 + 3) = 5$.

E: Simplify the exponents, $(5)^2 = 25$.

The equation now looks like this: $5 + 20 \div 4 \times 25 - 6$.

MD: Perform multiplication and division from left to right, $20 \div 4 = 5$; then $5 \times 25 = 125$.

The equation now looks like this: $5 + 125 - 6$.

AS: Perform addition and subtraction from left to right, $5 + 125 = 130$; then $130 - 6 = 124$.

The laws of exponents are as follows:

1. Any number to the power of 1 is equal to itself: $a^1 = a$.
2. The number 1 raised to any power is equal to 1: $1^n = 1$.
3. Any number raised to the power of 0 is equal to 1: $a^0 = 1$.
4. Add exponents to multiply powers of the same base number: $a^n \times a^m = a^{n+m}$.
5. Subtract exponents to divide powers of the same number; that is $a^n \div a^m = a^{n-m}$.
6. Multiply exponents to raise a power to a power: $(a^n)^m = a^{n \times m}$.
7. If multiplied or divided numbers inside parentheses are collectively raised to a power, this is the same as each individual term being raised to that power: $(a \times b)^n = a^n \times b^n$; $(a \div b)^n = a^n \div b^n$.

Note: Exponents do not have to be integers. Fractional or decimal exponents follow all the rules above as well.

Example: $5^{\frac{1}{4}} \times 5^{\frac{3}{4}} = 5^{\frac{1}{4}+\frac{3}{4}} = 5^1 = 5$.

A root, such as a square root, is another way of writing a fractional exponent. Instead of using a superscript, roots use the radical symbol ($\sqrt{}$) to indicate the operation. A radical will have a number underneath the bar, and may sometimes have a number in the upper left: $\sqrt[n]{a}$, read as "the nth root of a." The relationship between radical notation and exponent notation can be described by this equation: $\sqrt[n]{a} = a^{\frac{1}{n}}$. The two special cases of $n = 2$ and $n = 3$ are called square roots and cube roots. If there is no number to the upper left, it is understood to be a square root ($n = 2$). Nearly all of the roots you encounter will be square roots. A square root is the same as a number raised to the one-half power. When we say that a is the square root of b ($a = \sqrt{b}$), we mean that a multiplied by itself equals b: ($a \times a = b$).

A perfect square is a number that has an integer for its square root. There are 10 perfect squares from 1 to 100: 1, 4, 9, 16, 25, 36, 49, 64, 81, 100 (the squares of integers 1 through 10).

Scientific notation is a way of writing large numbers in a shorter form. The form $a \times 10^n$ is used in scientific notation, where a is greater than or equal to 1, but less than 10, and n is the number of places the decimal must move to get from the original number to a. *Example*: The number 230,400,000 is cumbersome to write. To write the value in scientific notation, place a decimal point between the first and second numbers, and include all digits through the last non-zero digit ($a = 2.304$). To find the appropriate power of 10, count the number of places the decimal point had to move ($n = 8$). The number is positive if the decimal moved to the left, and negative if it moved to the right. We can then write 230,400,000 as 2.304×10^8. If we look instead at the number 0.00002304, we have the same value for a, but this time the decimal moved 5 places to the right ($n = -5$). Thus, 0.00002304 can be written as 2.304×10^{-5}. Using this notation makes it simple to compare very large or very small numbers. By comparing exponents, it is easy to see that 3.28×10^4 is smaller than 1.51×10^5, because 4 is less than 5.

Positive and Negative Numbers

A precursor to working with negative numbers is understanding what **absolute values** are. A number's absolute value is simply the distance away from zero a number is on the number line. The absolute value of a number is always positive and is written $|x|$.

When adding signed numbers, if the signs are the same simply add the absolute values of the addends and apply the original sign to the sum. For example, $(+4) + (+8) = +12$ and $(-4) + (-8) = -12$. When the original signs are different, take the absolute values of the addends and subtract the smaller value from the larger value, then apply the original sign of the larger value to the difference. For instance, $(+4) + (-8) = -4$ and $(-4) + (+8) = +4$.

For subtracting signed numbers, change the sign of the number after the minus symbol and then follow the same rules used for addition. For example, $(+4) - (+8) = (+4) + (-8) = -4$.

If the signs are the same the product is positive when multiplying signed numbers. For example, $(+4) \times (+8) = +32$ and $(-4) \times (-8) = +32$. If the signs are opposite, the product is negative. For example, $(+4) \times (-8) = -32$ and $(-4) \times (+8) = -32$. When more than two factors are multiplied together, the sign of the product is determined by how many negative factors are present. If there are an odd number of negative factors then the product is negative, whereas an even number of negative factors indicates a positive product. For instance, $(+4) \times (-8) \times (-2) = +64$ and $(-4) \times (-8) \times (-2) = -64$.

The rules for dividing signed numbers are similar to multiplying signed numbers. If the dividend and divisor have the same sign, the quotient is positive. If the dividend and divisor have opposite signs, the quotient is negative. For example, $(-4) \div (+8) = -0.5$.

Factors and Multiples

Factors are numbers that are multiplied together to obtain a product. For example, in the equation $2 \times 3 = 6$, the numbers 2 and 3 are factors. A prime number has only two factors (1 and itself), but other numbers can have many factors.

A common factor is a number that divides exactly into two or more other numbers. For example, the factors of 12 are 1, 2, 3, 4, 6, and 12, while the factors of 15 are 1, 3, 5, and 15. The common factors of 12 and 15 are 1 and 3. A prime factor is also a prime number. Therefore, the prime factors of 12 are 2 and 3. For 15, the prime factors are 3 and 5.

The greatest common factor (GCF) is the largest number that is a factor of two or more numbers. For example, the factors of 15 are 1, 3, 5, and 15; the factors of 35 are 1, 5, 7, and 35. Therefore, the greatest common factor of 15 and 35 is 5.

Review Video: Greatest Common Factor (GCF)
Visit mometrix.com/academy and enter code: 838699

The least common multiple (LCM) is the smallest number that is a multiple of two or more numbers. For example, the multiples of 3 include 3, 6, 9, 12, 15, etc.; the multiples of 5 include 5, 10, 15, 20, etc. Therefore, the least common multiple of 3 and 5 is 15.

Fractions, Percentages, and Related Concepts

A fraction is a number that is expressed as one integer written above another integer, with a dividing line between them $\left(\frac{x}{y}\right)$. It represents the quotient of the two numbers "x divided by y." It can also be thought of as x out of y equal parts.

The top number of a fraction is called the numerator, and it represents the number of parts under consideration. The 1 in $\frac{1}{4}$ means that 1 part out of the whole is being considered in the calculation. The bottom number of a fraction is called the denominator, and it represents the total number of equal parts. The 4 in $\frac{1}{4}$ means that the whole consists of 4 equal parts. A fraction cannot have a denominator of zero; this is referred to as "undefined."

Review Video: <u>Fractions</u>
Visit mometrix.com/academy and enter code: 262335

Fractions can be manipulated, without changing the value of the fraction, by multiplying or dividing (but not adding or subtracting) both the numerator and denominator by the same number. If you divide both numbers by a common factor, you are reducing or simplifying the fraction. Two fractions that have the same value, but are expressed differently are known as equivalent fractions. For example, $\frac{2}{10}, \frac{3}{15}, \frac{4}{20}$, and $\frac{5}{25}$ are all equivalent fractions. They can also all be reduced or simplified to $\frac{1}{5}$.

When two fractions are manipulated so that they have the same denominator, this is known as finding a common denominator. The number chosen to be that common denominator should be the least common multiple of the two original denominators. *Example:* $\frac{3}{4}$ and $\frac{5}{6}$; the least common multiple of 4 and 6 is 12. Manipulating to achieve the common denominator: $\frac{3}{4} = \frac{9}{12}; \frac{5}{6} = \frac{10}{12}$.

If two fractions have a common denominator, they can be added or subtracted simply by adding or subtracting the two numerators and retaining the same denominator. *Example:* $\frac{1}{2} + \frac{1}{4} = \frac{2}{4} + \frac{1}{4} = \frac{3}{4}$. If the two fractions do not already have the same denominator, one or both of them must be manipulated to achieve a common denominator before they can be added or subtracted.

Two fractions can be multiplied by multiplying the two numerators to find the new numerator and the two denominators to find the new denominator.

Example: $\frac{1}{3} \times \frac{2}{3} = \frac{1 \times 2}{3 \times 3} = \frac{2}{9}$.

Review Video: <u>Multiplying Fractions</u>
Visit mometrix.com/academy and enter code: 638849

Two fractions can be divided by flipping the numerator and denominator of the second fraction and then proceeding as though it were a multiplication. *Example:* $\frac{2}{3} \div \frac{3}{4} = \frac{2}{3} \times \frac{4}{3} = \frac{8}{9}$.

Review Video: <u>Dividing Fractions</u>
Visit mometrix.com/academy and enter code: 300874

A fraction whose denominator is greater than its numerator is known as a proper fraction, while a fraction whose numerator is greater than its denominator is known as an improper fraction. Proper fractions have values less than one and improper fractions have values greater than one.

A mixed number is a number that contains both an integer and a fraction. Any improper fraction can be rewritten as a mixed number. *Example*: $\frac{8}{3} = \frac{6}{3} + \frac{2}{3} = 2 + \frac{2}{3} = 2\frac{2}{3}$. Similarly, any mixed number can be rewritten as an improper fraction. *Example*: $1\frac{3}{5} = 1 + \frac{3}{5} = \frac{5}{5} + \frac{3}{5} = \frac{8}{5}$.

Percentages can be thought of as fractions that are based on a whole of 100; that is, one whole is equal to 100%. The word percent means "per hundred." Fractions can be expressed as percents by finding equivalent fractions with a denomination of 100. *Example*: $\frac{7}{10} = \frac{70}{100} = 70\%$; $\frac{1}{4} = \frac{25}{100} = 25\%$.

To express a percentage as a fraction, divide the percentage number by 100 and reduce the fraction to its simplest possible terms. *Example*: $60\% = \frac{60}{100} = \frac{3}{5}$; $96\% = \frac{96}{100} = \frac{24}{25}$.

Converting decimals to percentages and percentages to decimals is as simple as moving the decimal point. To convert from a decimal to a percent, move the decimal point two places to the right. To convert from a percent to a decimal, move it two places to the left. *Example*: 0.23 = 23%; 5.34 = 534%; 0.007 = 0.7%; 700% = 7.00; 86% = 0.86; 0.15% = 0.0015.

It may be helpful to remember that the percentage number will always be larger than the equivalent decimal number.

A percentage problem can be presented three main ways: (1) Find what percentage of some number another number is. *Example*: What percentage of 40 is 8? (2) Find what number is some percentage of a given number. *Example*: What number is 20% of 40? (3) Find what number another number is a given percentage of. *Example*: What number is 8 20% of? The three components in all of these cases are the same: a whole (W), a part (P), and a percentage (%). These are related by the equation: $P = W \times \%$. This is the form of the equation you would use to solve problems of type (2). To solve types (1) and (3), you would use these two forms: $\% = \frac{P}{W}$ and $W = \frac{P}{\%}$.

The thing that frequently makes percentage problems difficult is that they are most often also word problems, so a large part of solving them is figuring out which quantities are what. Here's an example: *In a school cafeteria, 7 students choose pizza, 9 choose hamburgers, and 4 choose tacos. Find the percentage that chooses tacos.* To find the whole, you must first add all of the parts: 7 + 9 + 4 = 20. The percentage can then be found by dividing the part by the whole($\% = \frac{P}{W}$): $\frac{4}{20} = \frac{20}{100} = 20\%$.

A ratio is a comparison of two quantities in a particular order. *Example*: If there are 14 computers in a lab, and the class has 20 students, there is a student to computer ratio of 20 to 14, commonly written as 20:14. Ratios are normally reduced to their smallest whole number representation, so 20:14 would be reduced to 10:7 by dividing both sides by 2.

A proportion is a relationship between two quantities that dictates how one changes when the other changes. A direct proportion describes a relationship in which a quantity increases by a set amount for every increase in the other quantity, or decreases by that same amount for every decrease in the other quantity. *Example*: Assuming a constant driving speed, the time required for a car trip increases as the distance of the trip increases. The distance to be traveled and the time required to travel are directly proportional.

Inverse proportion is a relationship in which an increase in one quantity is accompanied by a decrease in the other, or vice versa. *Example*: the time required for a car trip decreases as the speed increases, and increases as the speed decreases, so the time required is inversely proportional to the speed of the car.

Systems of Equations

Systems of Equations are a set of simultaneous equations that all use the same variables. A solution to a system of equations must be true for each equation in the system. *Consistent Systems* are those with at least one solution. *Inconsistent Systems* are systems of equations that have no solution.

Review Video: Systems of Equations
Visit mometrix.com/academy and enter code: 658153

To solve a system of linear equations by *substitution*, start with the easier equation and solve for one of the variables. Express this variable in terms of the other variable. Substitute this expression in the other equation, and solve for the other variable. The solution should be expressed in the form (x, y). Substitute the values into both of the original equations to check your answer. Consider the following problem.

Solve the system using substitution:

$$x + 6y = 15$$
$$3x - 12y = 18$$

Solve the first equation for x:

$$x = 15 - 6y$$

Substitute this value in place of x in the second equation, and solve for y:

$$3(15 - 6y) - 12y = 18$$
$$45 - 18y - 12y = 18$$
$$30y = 27$$
$$y = \frac{27}{30} = \frac{9}{10} = 0.9$$

Plug this value for y back into the first equation to solve for x:

$$x = 15 - 6(0.9) = 15 - 5.4 = 9.6$$

Check both equations if you have time:

$$9.6 + 6(0.9) = 9.6 + 5.4 = 15$$
$$3(9.6) - 12(0.9) = 28.8 - 10.8 = 18$$

Therefore, the solution is $(9.6, 0.9)$.

To solve a system of equations using *elimination*, begin by rewriting both equations in standard form $Ax + By = C$. Check to see if the coefficients of one pair of like variables add to zero. If not, multiply one or both of the equations by a non-zero number to make one set of like variables add to zero. Add the two equations to solve for one of the variables. Substitute this value into one of the original equations to solve for the other variable. Check your work by substituting into the other equation. Next we will solve the same problem as above, but using the addition method.

Solve the system using elimination:

$$x + 6y = 15$$
$$3x - 12y = 18$$

If we multiply the first equation by 2, we can eliminate the y terms:

$$2x + 12y = 30$$
$$3x - 12y = 18$$

Add the equations together and solve for x:

$$5x = 48$$
$$x = \frac{48}{5} = 9.6$$

Plug the value for x back into either of the original equations and solve for y:

$$9.6 + 6y = 15$$
$$y = \frac{15 - 9.6}{6} = 0.9$$

Check both equations if you have time:

$$9.6 + 6(0.9) = 9.6 + 5.4 = 15$$
$$3(9.6) - 12(0.9) = 28.8 - 10.8 = 18$$

Therefore, the solution is $(9.6, 0.9)$.

Polynomial Algebra

To multiply two binomials, follow the *FOIL* method. FOIL stands for:

F = First: Multiply the first term of each binomial
O = Outer: Multiply the outer terms of each binomial
I = Inner: Multiply the inner terms of each binomial
L = Last: Multiply the last term of each binomial

Using FOIL, $(Ax + By)(Cx + Dy) = ACx^2 + ADxy + BCxy + BDy^2$.

Review Video: Multiplying Terms Using the FOIL Method
Visit mometrix.com/academy and enter code: 854792

To divide polynomials, begin by arranging the terms of each polynomial in order of one variable. You may arrange in ascending or descending order, but be consistent with both polynomials. To get the first term of the quotient, divide the first term of the dividend by the first term of the divisor. Multiply the first term of the quotient by the entire divisor and subtract that product from the dividend. Repeat for the second and successive terms until you either get a remainder of zero or a remainder whose degree is less than the degree of the divisor. If the quotient has a remainder, write the answer as a mixed expression in the form: $\text{quotient} + \frac{\text{remainder}}{\text{divisor}}$.

Rational Expressions are fractions with polynomials in both the numerator and the denominator; the value of the polynomial in the denominator cannot be equal to zero. To add or subtract rational expressions, first find the common denominator, then rewrite each fraction as an equivalent fraction with the common denominator. Finally, add or subtract the numerators to get the numerator of the answer, and keep the common denominator as the denominator of the answer. When multiplying rational expressions, factor each polynomial and cancel like factors (a factor which appears in both the numerator and the denominator). Then, multiply all remaining factors in the numerator to get the numerator of the product, and multiply the remaining factors in the denominator to get the denominator of the product. Remember – cancel entire factors, not individual terms. To divide rational expressions, take the reciprocal of the divisor (the rational expression you are dividing by) and multiply by the dividend.

> **Review Video: Rational Expressions**
> Visit mometrix.com/academy and enter code: 415183

Below are patterns of some special products to remember: *perfect trinomial squares*, the *difference between two squares*, the *sum and difference of two cubes*, and *perfect cubes*.

- Perfect Trinomial Squares: $x^2 + 2xy + y^2 = (x + y)^2$ or $x^2 - 2xy + y^2 = (x - y)^2$
- Difference between Two Squares: $x^2 - y^2 = (x + y)(x - y)$
- Sum of Two Cubes: $x^3 + y^3 = (x + y)(x^2 - xy + y^2)$
  Note: the second factor is NOT the same as a perfect trinomial square, so do not try to factor it further.
- Difference between Two Cubes: $x^3 - y^3 = (x - y)(x^2 + xy + y^2)$
  Again, the second factor is NOT the same as a perfect trinomial square.
- Perfect Cubes: $x^3 + 3x^2y + 3xy^2 + y^3 = (x + y)^3$ and $x^3 - 3x^2y + 3xy^2 - y^3 = (x - y)^3$

In order to *factor* a polynomial, first check for a common monomial factor. When the greatest common monomial factor has been factored out, look for patterns of special products: differences of two squares, the sum or difference of two cubes for binomial factors, or perfect trinomial squares for trinomial factors. If the factor is a trinomial but not a perfect trinomial square, look for a factorable form, such as $x^2 + (a + b)x + ab = (x + a)(x + b)$ or $(ac)x^2 + (ad + bc)x + bd = (ax + b)(cx + d)$. For factors with four terms, look for groups to factor. Once you have found the factors, write the original polynomial as the product of all the factors. Make sure all of the polynomial factors are prime. Monomial factors may be prime or composite. Check your work by multiplying the factors to make sure you get the original polynomial.

Solving Quadratic Equations

The *Quadratic Formula* is used to solve quadratic equations when other methods are more difficult. To use the quadratic formula to solve a quadratic equation, begin by rewriting the equation in standard form $ax^2 + bx + c = 0$, where a, b, and c are coefficients. Once you have identified the values of the coefficients, substitute those values into the quadratic formula $= \frac{-b \pm \sqrt{b^2 - 4ac}}{2a}$. Evaluate the equation and simplify the expression. Again, check each root by substituting into the original equation. In the quadratic formula, the portion of the formula under the radical ($b^2 - 4ac$) is called the *Discriminant*. If the discriminant is zero, there is only one root: zero. If the discriminant is positive, there are two different real roots. If the discriminant is negative, there are no real roots.

To solve a quadratic equation by *Factoring*, begin by rewriting the equation in standard form, if necessary. Factor the side with the variable then set each of the factors equal to zero and solve the resulting linear equations. Check your answers by substituting the roots you found into the original equation. If, when writing the equation in standard form, you have an equation in the form $x^2 + c = 0$ or $x^2 - c = 0$, set $x^2 = -c$ or $x^2 = c$ and take the square root of c. If $c = 0$, the only real root is zero. If c is positive, there are two real roots—the positive and negative square root values. If c is negative, there are no real roots because you cannot take the square root of a negative number.

To solve a quadratic equation by *Completing the Square*, rewrite the equation so that all terms containing the variable are on the left side of the equal sign, and all the constants are on the right side of the equal sign. Make sure the coefficient of the squared term is 1. If there is a coefficient with the squared term, divide each term on both sides of the equal side by that number. Next, work with the coefficient of the single-variable term. Square half of this coefficient, and add that value to both sides. Now you can factor the left side (the side containing the variable) as the square of a binomial. $x^2 + 2ax + a^2 = C \Rightarrow$ $(x + a)^2 = C$, where x is the variable, and a and C are constants. Take the square root of both sides and solve for the variable. Substitute the value of the variable in the original problem to check your work.

Basic Geometry

ANGLES

An angle is formed when two lines or line segments meet at a common point. It may be a common starting point for a pair of segments or rays, or it may be the intersection of lines. Angles are represented by the symbol $\angle$.

The vertex is the point at which two segments or rays meet to form an angle. If the angle is formed by intersecting rays, lines, and/or line segments, the vertex is the point at which four angles are formed. The pairs of angles opposite one another are called vertical angles, and their measures are equal. In the figure below, angles ABC and DBE are congruent, as are angles ABD and CBE.

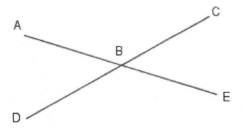

An acute angle is an angle with a degree measure less than 90°.

A right angle is an angle with a degree measure of exactly 90°.

An obtuse angle is an angle with a degree measure greater than 90° but less than 180°.

A straight angle is an angle with a degree measure of exactly 180°. This is also a semicircle.

A reflex angle is an angle with a degree measure greater than 180° but less than 360°.

A full angle is an angle with a degree measure of exactly 360°.

Two angles whose sum is exactly 90° are said to be complementary. The two angles may or may not be adjacent. In a right triangle, the two acute angles are complementary.

Two angles whose sum is exactly 180° are said to be supplementary. The two angles may or may not be adjacent. Two intersecting lines always form two pairs of supplementary angles. Adjacent supplementary angles will always form a straight line.

CIRCLES

The center is the single point inside the circle that is equidistant from every point on the circle. (Point O in the diagram below.)

The radius is a line segment that joins the center of the circle and any one point on the circle. All radii of a circle are equal. (Segments OX, OY, and OZ in the diagram below.)

The diameter is a line segment that passes through the center of the circle and has both endpoints on the circle. The length of the diameter is exactly twice the length of the radius. (Segment XZ in the diagram below.)

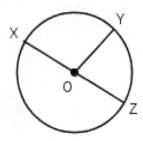

TRIANGLES

A triangle is a polygon with three sides and three angles. Triangles can be classified according to the length of their sides or magnitude of their angles.

An acute triangle is a triangle whose three angles are all less than 90°. If two of the angles are equal, the acute triangle is also an isosceles triangle. If the three angles are all equal, the acute triangle is also an equilateral triangle.

A right triangle is a triangle with exactly one angle equal to 90°. All right triangles follow the Pythagorean Theorem. A right triangle can never be acute or obtuse.

An obtuse triangle is a triangle with exactly one angle greater than 90°. The other two angles may or may not be equal. If the two remaining angles are equal, the obtuse triangle is also an isosceles triangle.

An equilateral triangle is a triangle with three congruent sides. An equilateral triangle will also have three congruent angles, each 60°. All equilateral triangles are also acute triangles.

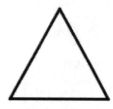

An isosceles triangle is a triangle with two congruent sides. An isosceles triangle will also have two congruent angles opposite the two congruent sides.

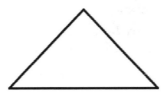

A scalene triangle is a triangle with no congruent sides. A scalene triangle will also have three angles of different measures. The angle with the largest measure is opposite the longest side, and the angle with the smallest measure is opposite the shortest side.

The Triangle Inequality Theorem states that the sum of the measures of any two sides of a triangle is always greater than the measure of the third side. If the sum of the measures of two sides were equal to the third side, a triangle would be impossible because the two sides would lie flat across the third side and there would be no vertex. If the sum of the measures of two of the sides was less than the third side, a closed figure would be impossible because the two shortest sides would never meet.

Similar triangles are triangles whose corresponding angles are congruent to one another. Their corresponding sides may or may not be equal, but they are proportional to one another. Since the angles in a triangle always sum to 180°, it is only necessary to determine that two pairs of corresponding angles are congruent, since the third will be also in that case.

Congruent triangles are similar triangles whose corresponding sides are all equal. Congruent triangles can be made to fit on top of one another by rotation, reflection, and/or translation. When trying to determine whether two triangles are congruent, there are several criteria that can be used.

AREA FORMULAS

Rectangle: $A = wl$, where w is the width and l is the length

Square: $A = s^2$, where s is the length of a side.

Triangle: $A = \frac{1}{2}bh$, where b is the length of one side (base) and h is the distance from that side to the opposite vertex measured perpendicularly (height).

Circle: $A = \pi r^2$, where π is the mathematical constant approximately equal to 3.14 and r is the distance from the center of the circle to any point on the circle (radius).

VOLUME FORMULAS

Rectangular Prism – all 6 sides are rectangles. The volume can be calculated as $V = s_1 \times s_2 \times s_3$, or the lengths of the three different sides multiplied together.

Cube – a special type of prism in which all faces are squares. The volume can be calculated as $V = s^3$, where s is the length of any side.

Sphere – a round solid consisting of one continuous, uniformly-curved surface. The volume can be calculated as $V = \frac{4}{3}\pi r^3$, where r is the distance from the center of the sphere to any point on the surface (radius).

Reading Comprehension Test

Possessing excellent reading skills is a necessity for anyone hoping to become a military aviator. The Reading Comprehension section of the ASTB-E is designed to measure your abilities in this area.

This section tests your ability to read and understand written passages of the level of difficulty you can expect to encounter in your aviation training and career. Many of the passages used in our practice test were taken directly from a helicopter operation instructional material.

You've probably taken numerous tests of reading comprehension in your educational career, and may have already identified the strategy that works best for you. If that's the case, you can go ahead and skip this next section. We're going to outline some of the strategies that we've found to be effective, but the key is finding the one or ones that work best for you.

Strategies

READ THE QUESTION(S) BEFORE READING THE PASSAGE

By identifying what you need to look for ahead of time, you can more quickly read the passage to find the information you need. In addition, reading the question will give you an idea of its complexity. If the question is simply asking you to find a detail in a passage, it probably won't take nearly as long as a question that requires you to make a conclusion about a hypothetical scenario. If it looks like the question will be very time-consuming, you can skip it and come back.

SYSTEMATICALLY ELIMINATE ANSWERS THAT ARE OBVIOUSLY WRONG

This will make it easier to focus on the remaining choices, and more importantly, you will improve your chances of correctly answering the question if you have to randomly guess.

USE CONTEXT CLUES TO UNDERSTAND DIFFICULT WORDS

You may encounter words and phrases that are new to you, and whose meanings you must decipher in order to answer a question correctly. If you don't know what they mean, you will have to use clues in the sentence to understand their meaning.

One effective way to handle unknown words is to highlight or circle them in the passage, and underline other words in the passage that provide clues to their meaning. As an example, try to use context clues figure out what the word "contraindicate" means in the sentence below:

> *Although Inventium is normally prescribed to relieve severe pain, a history of liver damage in a patient contraindicates its use.*

Even if you don't know what "contraindicates" means, you can still figure it out from the rest of the sentence. The word "although" is key because it signals contrasting ideas. In the sentence above, we know that there's a (fictional) medicine, Inventium, that's prescribed to relieve pain. The word "although" tells us that even though Inventium is **normally** prescribed to relieve severe pain, there are some situations in which that wouldn't happen, and the second part of the sentence completes the puzzle: you wouldn't prescribe Inventium if a patient has a history of liver damage. Thus, even if you don't recognize the word "contraindicate," you can deduce that it means to signal somebody to *not* do something—in this case, liver damage signals a doctor to not prescribe a particular medicine.

General Reading Comprehension Skills

TOPICS AND MAIN IDEAS

One of the most important skills in reading comprehension is the identification of **topics** and **main ideas.** There is a subtle difference between these two features. The topic is the subject of a text (i.e., what the text is all about). The main idea, on the other hand, is the most important point being made by the author. The topic is usually expressed in a few words at the most while the main idea often needs a full sentence to be completely defined. As an example, a short passage might have the topic of penguins and the main idea could be written as *Penguins are different from other birds in many ways.* In most nonfiction writing, the topic and the main idea will be stated directly and often appear in a sentence at the very beginning or end of the text. When being tested on an understanding of the author's topic, you may be able to skim the passage for the general idea, by reading only the first sentence of each paragraph. A body paragraph's first sentence is often--but not always--the main topic sentence which gives you a summary of the content in the paragraph.

However, there are cases in which the reader must figure out an unstated topic or main idea. In these instances, you must read every sentence of the text and try to come up with an overarching idea that is supported by each of those sentences.

> **Review Video: Topics and Main Ideas**
> Visit mometrix.com/academy and enter code: 407801

SUPPORTING DETAILS

Supporting details provide evidence and backing for the main point. In order to show that a main idea is correct, or valid, authors add details that help prove their point. All texts contain details, but they are only classified as supporting details when they serve to reinforce some larger point. Supporting details are most commonly found in informative and persuasive texts. In some cases, they will be clearly indicated with terms like *for example* or *for instance*, or they will be enumerated with terms like *first*, *second*, and *last*. However, you need to be prepared for texts that do not contain those indicators. As a reader, you should consider whether the author's supporting details really back up his or her main point. Supporting details can be factual and correct, yet they may not be relevant to the author's point. Conversely, supporting details can seem pertinent, but they can be ineffective because they are based on opinion or assertions that cannot be proven.

TOPIC AND SUMMARY SENTENCES

Topic and summary sentences are a convenient way to encapsulate the main idea of a text. In some textbooks and academic articles, the author will place a topic or summary sentence at the beginning of each section as a means of preparing the reader for what is to come. Research suggests that the brain is more receptive to new information when it has been prepared by the presentation of the main idea or some key words. The phenomenon is somewhat akin to the primer coat of paint that allows subsequent coats of paint to absorb more easily. A good topic sentence will be clear and not contain any jargon. When topic or summary sentences are not provided, good readers can jot down their own so that they can find their place in a text and refresh their memory.

PREDICTIONS BASED ON PRIOR KNOWLEDGE

A prediction is a guess about what will happen next. Readers constantly make predictions based on what they have read and what they already know. Consider the following sentence: *Staring at the computer screen in shock, Kim blindly reached over for the brimming glass of water on the shelf to her side.* The sentence suggests that Kim is agitated, and that she is not looking at the glass that she is going to pick up. So, a reader might predict that Kim is going to knock over the glass. Of course, not every prediction will be accurate: perhaps Kim will pick the glass up cleanly. Nevertheless, the author has certainly created the expectation that the water might be spilled. Predictions are always subject to revision as the reader acquires more information.

MAKING INFERENCES

Readers are often required to understand a text that claims and suggests ideas without stating them directly. An **inference** is a piece of information that is implied but not written outright by the author. For instance, consider the following sentence: *After the final out of the inning, the fans were filled with joy and rushed the field.* From this sentence, a reader can infer that the fans were watching a baseball game and their team won the game. Readers should take great care to avoid using information beyond the provided passage before making inferences. As you practice with drawing inferences, you will find that they require concentration and attention.

DRAWING CONCLUSIONS

In addition to inference and prediction, readers must often **draw conclusions** about the information they have read. When asked for a *conclusion* that may be drawn, look for critical "hedge" phrases, such as *likely*, *may*, *can*, *will often*, among many others. When you are being tested on this knowledge, remember the question that writers insert into these hedge phrases to cover every possibility. Often an answer will be wrong simply because there is no room for exception. Extreme positive or negative answers (such as always or never) are usually not correct. You **should not** rely on any outside knowledge that is not gathered from the passage to answer the related questions. Correct answers can be derived straight from the passage.

SEQUENCE

Readers must be able to identify a text's **sequence**, or the order in which things happen. Often, when the sequence is very important to the author, the text is indicated with signal words like *first*, *then*, *next*, and *last*. However, a sequence can be merely implied and must be noted by the reader. Consider the sentence *He walked through the garden and gave water and fertilizer to the plants.* Clearly, the man did not walk through the garden before he collected water and fertilizer for the plants. So, the implied sequence is that he first collected water and fertilizer, next he walked through the garden, and last he gave water or fertilizer as necessary to the plants.

Texts do not always proceed in an orderly sequence from first to last. Sometimes they begin at the end and start over at the beginning. As a reader, you can enhance your understanding of the passage by taking brief notes to clarify the sequence.

COMPARISON AND CONTRAST

Authors will use different stylistic and writing devices to make their meaning clear for readers. One of those devices is comparison and contrast. As mentioned previously, when an author describes the ways in which two things are alike, he or she is comparing them. When the author describes the ways in which two things are different, he or she is contrasting them. The "compare and contrast" essay is one of the most common forms in nonfiction. These passages are often signaled with certain words: a comparison may have indicating terms such as *both, same, like, too,* and *as well*; while a contrast may have terms like *but, however, on the other hand, instead,* and *yet.* Of course, comparisons and contrasts may be implicit without using any such signaling language. A single sentence may both compare and contrast. Consider the sentence *Brian and Sheila love ice cream, but Brian prefers vanilla and Sheila prefers strawberry.* In one sentence, the author has described both a similarity (love of ice cream) and a difference (favorite flavor).

CAUSE AND EFFECT

One of the most common text structures is cause and effect. A cause is an act or event that makes something happen, and an effect is the thing that happens as a result of the cause. A cause-and-effect relationship is not always explicit, but there are some terms in English that signal causes, such as *since, because,* and *due to.* Furthermore, terms that signal effects include *consequently, therefore, this lead(s) to.* As an example, consider the sentence *Because the sky was clear, Ron did not bring an umbrella.* The cause is the clear sky, and the effect is that Ron did not bring an umbrella. However, readers may find that sometimes the cause-and-effect relationship will not be clearly noted. For instance, the sentence *He was late and missed the meeting* does not contain any signaling words, but the sentence still contains a cause (he was late) and an effect (he missed the meeting).

IDENTIFYING AN AUTHOR'S POSITION

In order to be an effective reader, one must pay attention to the author's **position** and purpose. Even those texts that seem objective and impartial, like textbooks, have a position and bias. Readers need to take these positions into account when considering the author's message. When an author uses emotional language or clearly favors one side of an argument, his or her position is clear. However, the author's position may be evident not only in what he or she writes, but also in what he or she doesn't write. In a normal setting, a reader would want to review some other texts on the same topic in order to develop a view of the author's position. If this was not possible, then you would want to acquire some background about the author. However, since you are in the middle of an exam and the only source of information is the text, you should look for language and argumentation that seems to indicate a particular stance on the subject.

PURPOSE

Usually, identifying the **purpose** of an author is easier than identifying his or her position. In most cases, the author has no interest in hiding his or her purpose. A text that is meant to entertain, for instance, should be written to please the reader. Most narratives, or stories, are written to entertain, though they may also inform or persuade. Informative texts are easy to identify, while the most difficult purpose of a text to identify is persuasion because the author has an interest in making this purpose hard to detect. When a reader discovers that the author is trying to persuade, he or she should be skeptical of the argument. For this reason persuasive texts often try to establish an entertaining tone and hope to amuse the reader into agreement. On the other hand, an informative tone may be implemented to create an appearance of authority and objectivity.

An author's purpose is evident often in the organization of the text (e.g., section headings in bold font points to an informative text). However, you may not have such organization available to you in your exam. Instead, if the author makes his or her main idea clear from the beginning, then the likely purpose of the text is to inform. If the author begins by making a claim and provides various arguments to support that claim, then the purpose is probably to persuade. If the author tells a story or seems to want the attention of the reader more than to push a particular point or deliver information, then his or her purpose is most likely to entertain. As a reader, you must judge authors on how well they accomplish their purpose. In other words, you need to consider the type of passage (e.g., technical, persuasive, etc.) that the author has written and if the author has followed the requirements of the passage type.

WORD MEANING FROM CONTEXT

One of the benefits of reading is the expansion of one's vocabulary. In order to obtain this benefit, however, one needs to know how to identify the definition of a word from its context. This means defining a word based on the words around it and the way it is used in a sentence. Consider the following sentence: *The elderly scholar spent his evenings hunched over arcane texts that few other people even knew existed.* The adjective *arcane* is uncommon, but you can obtain significant information about it based on its use in the sentence. The fact that few other people know of their existence allows you to assume that "arcane texts" must be rare and be of interest to a few people. Also, the texts are being read by an elderly scholar. So, you can assume that they focus on difficult academic subjects. Sometimes, words can be defined by what they are not. Consider the following sentence: *Ron's fealty to his parents was not shared by Karen, who disobeyed their every command.* Someone who disobeys is not demonstrating *fealty*. So, you can infer that the word means something like *obedience* or *respect*.

IDENTIFYING THE LOGICAL CONCLUSION

Identifying a logical conclusion can help you determine whether you agree with the writer or not. Coming to this conclusion is much like making an inference: the approach requires you to combine the information given by the text with what you already know in order to make a logical conclusion. If the author intended the reader to draw a certain conclusion, then you can expect the author's argumentation and detail to be leading in that direction. One way to approach the task of drawing conclusions is to make brief notes of all the points made by the author. When the notes are arranged on paper, they may clarify the logical conclusion. Another way to approach conclusions is to consider whether the reasoning of the author raises any pertinent questions. Sometimes you will be able to draw several conclusions from a passage. On occasion these will be conclusions that were never imagined by the author. Therefore, be aware that these conclusions must be supported directly by the text.

Review Video: Identifying Logical Conclusions
Visit mometrix.com/academy and enter code: 281653

Mechanical Comprehension Test

The Mechanical Comprehension Test (MCT) isn't as long as the Math Skills or Reading Comprehension sections. It has a time limit of only 15 minutes. Keep in mind that this section is computer adaptive like the Math Skills subtest. Once again, this means that there is no fixed number of questions on the test. The questions get progressively harder each time you answer a question correctly, and progressively easier each time you answer a question incorrectly. This is an ongoing process throughout the test, and this format allows the computer software to tailor the questions to your current perceived skill level. Do not guess on this section unless you've exhausted all other options because incorrect answers will have a negative impact on your final score.

If you've ever taken the ASVAB, the Mechanical Comprehension subtest on the ASTB-E should not be all that foreign to you. The two tests cover a very similar breadth of concepts and in very similar ways. You'll see questions about gears, pulleys, levers, simple machines, mechanical advantage, and so on. Most questions in this section will be accompanied by a drawing to help illustrate the physical situation that is being asked about. None of the questions should baffle you, nor should any of them require knowledge of physics or mechanics beyond the high school level. The emphasis in Mechanical Comprehension is much more on aptitude and intuition than on acquired knowledge.

That is not to say that you shouldn't take an inventory of your knowledge and skills in physics and mechanics as part of your ASTB-E test preparation. On the contrary, developing a strong background in those areas is one of the best ways to make these concepts intuitive to you. If it has been a while since you've interacted with these topics on a regular basis, a refresher is probably in order. Since few applicants for military aviation training are engaged in the kind of jobs or academic studies which require them to rely on their knowledge of physics on a daily basis, we've included an extensive primer on all the basics that might show up on the ASTB-E.

Kinematics

To begin, we will look at the basics of physics. At its heart, physics is just a set of explanations for the ways in which matter and energy behave. There are three key concepts used to describe how matter moves:

1. Displacement
2. Velocity
3. Acceleration

DISPLACEMENT

Concept: where and how far an object has gone

Calculation: final position – initial position

When something changes its location from one place to another, it is said to have undergone displacement. If a golf ball is hit across a sloped green into the hole, the displacement only takes into account the final and initial locations, not the path of the ball.

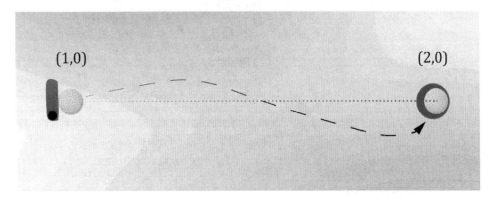

Displacement along a straight line is a very simple example of a vector quantity: that is, it has both a magnitude and a direction. Direction is as important as magnitude in many measurements. If we can determine the original and final position of the object, then we can determine the total displacement with this simple equation:

$$\textbf{Displacement } = \textbf{ final position } - \textbf{ original position}$$

The hole (final position) is at the Cartesian coordinate location (2, 0) and the ball is hit from the location (1, 0). The displacement is:

$$\text{Displacement} = (2,0) - (1,0)$$

$$\text{Displacement} = (1,0)$$

The displacement has a magnitude of 1 and a direction of the positive x direction.

VELOCITY

Concept: the rate of moving from one position to another

Calculation: change in position / change in time

Velocity answers the question, "How quickly is an object moving?" For example, if a car and a plane travel between two cities which are a hundred miles apart, but the car takes two hours and the plane takes one hour, the car has the same displacement as the plane, but a smaller velocity.

In order to solve some of the problems on the exam, you may need to assess the velocity of an object. If we want to calculate the average velocity of an object, we must know two things. First, we must know its displacement. Second, we must know the time it took to cover this distance. The formula for average velocity is quite simple:

$$\text{average velocity} = \frac{\text{displacement}}{\text{change in time}}$$

Or

$$\text{average velocity} = \frac{\text{final position} - \text{original position}}{\text{final time} - \text{original time}}$$

To complete the example, the velocity of the plane is calculated to be:

$$\text{plane average velocity} = \frac{100 \text{ miles}}{1 \text{ hour}} = 100 \text{ miles per hour}$$

The velocity of the car is less:

$$\text{car average velocity} = \frac{100 \text{ miles}}{2 \text{ hours}} = 50 \text{ miles per hour}$$

Often, people confuse the words *speed* and *velocity*. There is a significant difference. The average velocity is based on the amount of displacement, a vector. Alternately, the average speed is based on the distance covered or the path length. The equation for speed is:

$$\text{average speed} = \frac{\text{total distance traveled}}{\text{change in time}}$$

Notice that we used total distance and *not* change in position, because speed is path-dependent.

If the plane traveling between cities had needed to fly around a storm on its way, making the distance traveled 50 miles greater than the distance the car traveled, the plane would still have the same total displacement as the car.

The calculation for the speed: For this reason, average speed can be calculated:

$$\text{plane average speed} = \frac{150 \text{ miles}}{1 \text{ hour}} = 150 \text{ miles per hour}$$

$$\text{car average speed} = \frac{100 \text{ miles}}{2 \text{ hours}} = 50 \text{ miles per hour}$$

ACCELERATION

Concept: how quickly something changes from one velocity to another

Calculation: change in velocity / change in time

Acceleration is the rate of change of the velocity of an object. If a car accelerates from zero velocity to 60 miles per hour (88 feet per second) in two seconds, the car has an impressive acceleration. But if a car performs the same change in velocity in eight seconds, the acceleration is much lower and not as impressive.

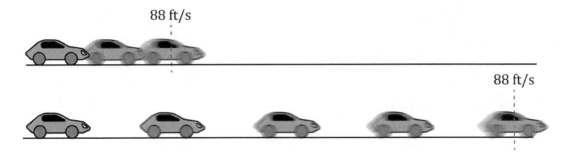

To calculate average acceleration, we may use the equation:

$$\textbf{average acceleration} = \frac{\textbf{change in velocity}}{\textbf{change in time}}$$

The acceleration of the cars is found to be:

$$\text{Car \#1 average acceleration} = \frac{88 \text{ feet per second}}{2 \text{ seconds}} = 44 \frac{\text{feet}}{\text{second}^2}$$

$$\text{Car \#2 average acceleration} = \frac{88 \text{ feet per second}}{8 \text{ seconds}} = 11 \frac{\text{feet}}{\text{second}^2}$$

Acceleration will be expressed in units of distance divided by time squared; for instance, meters per second squared or feet per second squared.

PROJECTILE MOTION

A specific application of the study of motion is projectile motion. Simple projectile motion occurs when an object is in the air and experiencing only the force of gravity. We will disregard drag for this topic. Some common examples of projectile motion are thrown balls, flying bullets, and falling rocks. The characteristics of projectile motion are:

1. The horizontal component of velocity doesn't change
2. The vertical acceleration due to gravity affects the vertical component of velocity

Because gravity only acts downwards, objects in projectile motion only experience acceleration in the y direction (vertical). The horizontal component of the object's velocity does not change in flight. This means that if a rock is thrown out off a cliff, the horizontal velocity, (think the shadow if the sun is directly overhead) will not change until the ball hits the ground.

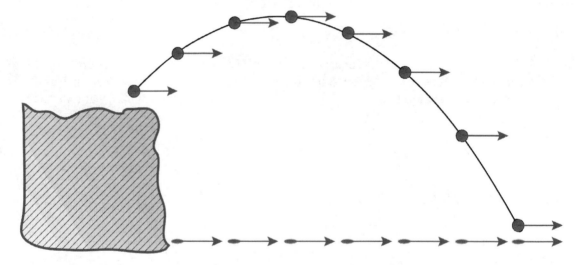

The velocity in the vertical direction is affected by gravity. Gravity imposes an acceleration of $g = 9.8 \frac{m}{s^2}$ or $32 \frac{ft}{s^2}$ downward on projectiles. The vertical component of velocity at any point is equal to:

$$\textbf{vertical velocity} = \textbf{original vertical velocity} - \textbf{g} \times \textbf{time}$$

When these characteristics are combined, there are three points of particular interest in a projectile's flight. At the beginning of a flight, the object has a horizontal component and a vertical component giving it a large speed. At the top of a projectile's flight, the vertical velocity equals zero, making the top the slowest part of travel. When the object passes the same height as the launch, the vertical velocity is opposite of the initial vertical velocity making the speed equal to the initial speed.

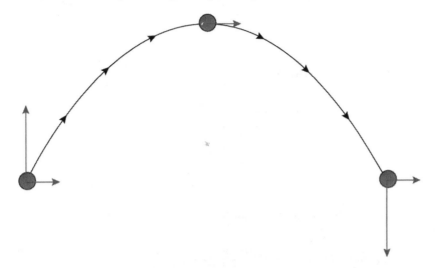

If the object continues falling below the initial height from which it was launched (e.g., it was launched from the edge of a cliff), it will have an even greater velocity than it did initially from that point until it hits the ground.

Rotational Kinematics

Concept: increasing the radius increases the linear speed

Calculation: linear speed $=$ radius $\times$ rotational speed

Another interesting application of the study of motion is rotation. In practice, simple rotation is when an object rotates around a point at a constant speed. Most questions covering rotational kinematics will provide the distance from a rotating object to the center of rotation (radius) and ask about the linear speed of the object. A point will have a greater linear speed when it is farther from the center of rotation.

If a potter is spinning his wheel at a constant speed of one revolution per second, the clay six inches away from the center will be going faster than the clay three inches from the center. The clay directly in the center of the wheel will not have any linear velocity.

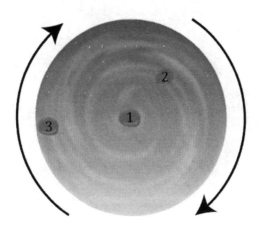

To find the linear speed of rotating objects using radians, we use the equation:

linear speed = (rotational speed [in radians]) × (radius)

Using degrees, the equation is:

$$\textbf{linear speed} = \textbf{(rotational speed [in degrees])} \times \frac{\boldsymbol{\pi} \textbf{ radians}}{\textbf{180 degrees}} \times \textbf{(radius)}$$

To find the speed of the pieces of clay we use the known values (rotational speed of 1 revolution per second, radii of 0 inches, 3 inches, and 6 inches) and the knowledge that one revolution = 2 pi.

$$clay\ \#1\ speed = \left(2\pi\frac{rad}{s}\right) \times (0\ inches) = 0\ \frac{inches}{second}$$

$$clay\ \#2\ speed = \left(2\pi\frac{rad}{s}\right) \times (3\ inches) = 18.8\ \frac{inches}{second}$$

$$clay\ \#3\ speed = \left(2\pi\frac{rad}{s}\right) \times (6\ inches) = 37.7\ \frac{inches}{second}$$

Review Video: <u>Linear Speed</u>
Visit mometrix.com/academy and enter code: 327101

CAMS

In the study of motion, a final application often tested is the cam. A cam and follower system allows mechanical systems to have timed, specified, and repeating motion. Although cams come in varied forms, tests focus on rotary cams. In engines, a cam shaft coordinates the valves for intake and exhaust. Cams are often used to convert rotational motion into repeating linear motion.

Cams rotate around one point. The follower sits on the edge of the cam and moves along with the edge. To understand simple cams, count the number of bumps on the cam. Each bump will cause the follower to move outwards.

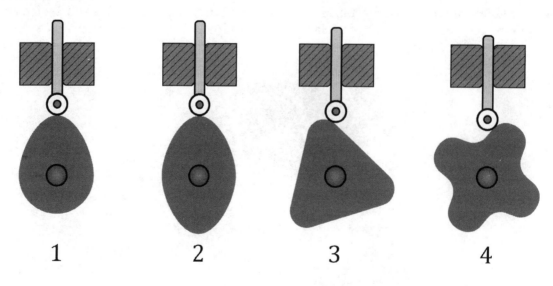

1 2 3 4

Another way to consider cams is to unravel the cam profile into a straight object. The follower will then follow the top of the profile.

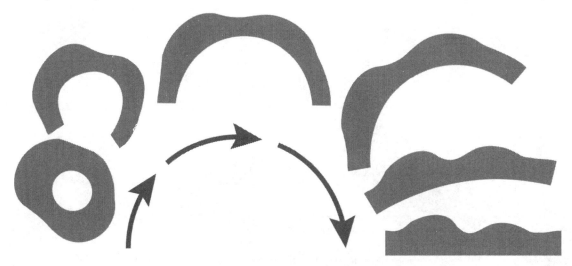

Kinetics

NEWTON'S THREE LAWS OF MECHANICS

The questions on the exam may require you to demonstrate familiarity with the concepts expressed in Newton's three laws of motion which relate to the concept of force.

Newton's first law – A body at rest will tend to remain at rest, while a body in motion will tend to remain in motion, unless acted upon by an external force.

Newton's second law – The acceleration of an object is directly proportional to the force being exerted on it and inversely proportional to its mass.

Newton's third law – For every force, there is an equal and opposite force.

FIRST LAW

Concept: Unless something interferes, an object won't start or stop moving

Although intuition supports the idea that objects do not start moving until a force acts on them, the idea of an object continuing forever without any forces can seem odd. Before Newton formulated his laws of mechanics, general thought held that some force had to act on an object continuously in order for it to move at a constant velocity. This seems to make sense: when an object is briefly pushed, it will eventually come to a stop. Newton, however, determined that unless some other force acted on the object (most notably friction or air resistance), it would continue in the direction it was pushed at the same velocity forever.

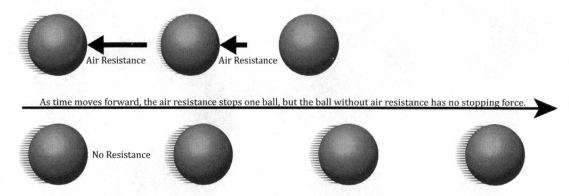

SECOND LAW

Concept: Acceleration increases linearly with force.

Although Newton's second law can be conceptually understood as a series of relationships describing how an increase in one factor will decrease another factor, the law can be understood best in equation format:

$$\text{Force} = \text{mass} \times \text{acceleration}$$

Or

$$\text{Acceleration} = \frac{\text{force}}{\text{mass}}$$

Or

$$\text{Mass} = \frac{\text{force}}{\text{acceleration}}$$

Each of the forms of the equation allows for a different look at the same relationships. To examine the relationships, change one factor and observe the result. If a steel ball, with a diameter of 6.3 cm, has a mass of 1 kg and an acceleration of 1 m/s^2, then the net force on the ball will be 1 Newton.

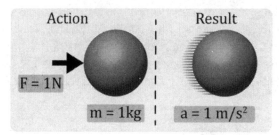

THIRD LAW

Concept: Nothing can push or pull without being pushed or pulled in return.

When any object exerts a force on another object, the other object exerts the opposite force back on the original object. To observe this, consider two spring-based fruit scales, both tipped on their sides as shown with the weighing surfaces facing each other. If fruit scale #1 is pressing fruit scale #2 into the wall, it exerts a force on fruit scale #2, measurable by the reading on scale #2. However, because fruit scale #1 is exerting a force on scale #2, scale #2 is exerting a force on scale #1 with an opposite direction, but the same magnitude.

FORCE

Concept: a push or pull on an object

Calculation: Force = mass × acceleration

A force is a vector which causes acceleration of a body. Force has both magnitude and direction. Furthermore, multiple forces acting on one object combine in vector addition. This can be demonstrated by considering an object placed at the origin of the coordinate plane. If it is pushed along the positive direction of the x-axis, it will move in this direction; if the force acting on it is in the positive direction of the y-axis, it will move in that direction. However, if both forces are applied at the same time, then the object will move at an angle to both the x and y axes, an angle determined by the relative amount of force exerted in each direction. In this way, we may see that the resulting force is a vector sum; that is, a net force that has both magnitude and direction.

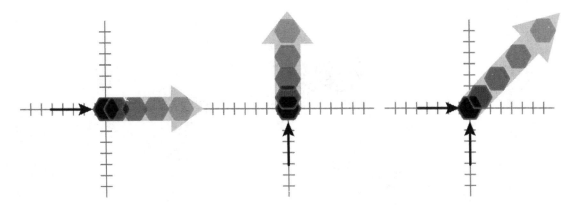

MASS

Concept: the amount of matter

Mass can be defined as the quantity of matter in an object. If we apply the same force to two objects of different mass, we will find that the resulting acceleration is different. Newton's Second Law of Motion describes the relationship between mass, force, and acceleration in the equation: ***Force = mass x*** *acceleration*. In other words, the acceleration of an object is directly proportional to the force being exerted on it and inversely proportional to its mass.

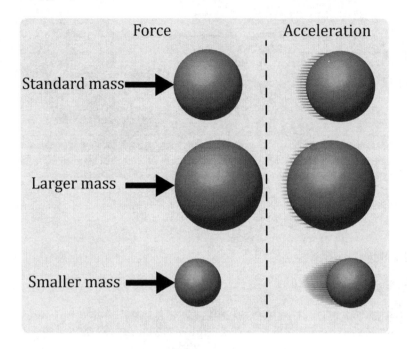

GRAVITY

Gravity is a force which exists between all objects with matter. Gravity is a pulling force between objects meaning that the forces on the objects point toward the opposite object. When Newton's third law is applied to gravity, the force pairs from gravity are shown to be equal in magnitude and opposite in direction.

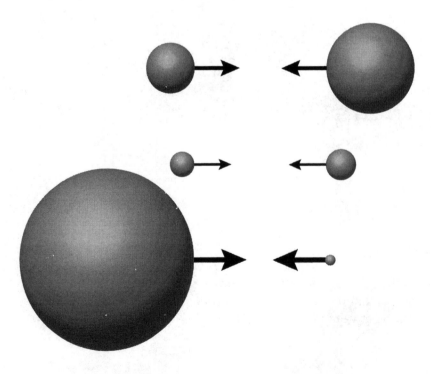

WEIGHT

Weight is sometimes confused with mass. While mass is the amount of matter, weight is the force exerted by the earth on an object with matter by gravity. The earth pulls every object of mass toward its center while every object of mass pulls the earth toward its center. The object's pull on the earth is equal in magnitude to the pull which the earth exerts, but, because the mass of the earth is very large in comparison (5.97×10^{24} kg), only the object appears to be affected by the force.

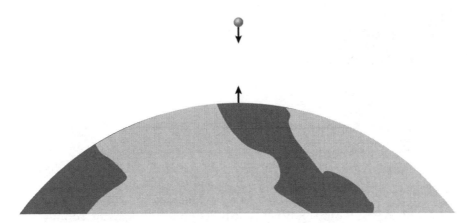

The gravity of earth causes a constant acceleration due to gravity (g) at a specific altitude. For most earthbound applications the acceleration due to gravity is 32.2 ft/s² or 9.8 m/s² in a downward direction. The equation for the force of gravity (weight) on an object is the equation from Newton's Second Law with the constant acceleration due to gravity (g).

$$\textbf{Force} = \textbf{mass} \times \textbf{acceleration}$$

$$\textbf{Weight} = \textbf{mass} \times \textbf{acceleration due to gravity}$$

$$\textbf{W} = \textbf{m} \times \textbf{g}$$

The SI (International Standard of Units) unit for weight is the Newton $\left(\frac{kg \times m}{s^2}\right)$. The English Engineering unit system uses the pound, or lb, as the unit for weight and force $\left(\frac{slug \times ft}{s^2}\right)$. Thus, a 2 kg object under the influence of gravity would have a weight of:

$$W = m \times g$$

$$W = 2 \text{ kg} \times 9.8 \frac{m}{s^2} = 19.6 \text{ N downwards}$$

NORMAL FORCE

Concept: the force perpendicular to a contact surface

The word "normal" is used in mathematics to mean perpendicular, and so the force known as normal force should be remembered as the perpendicular force exerted on an object that is resting on some other surface. For instance, if a box is resting on a horizontal surface, we may say that the normal force is directed upwards through the box (the opposite, downward force is the weight of the box). If the box is resting on a wedge, the normal force from the wedge is not vertical but is perpendicular to the wedge edge.

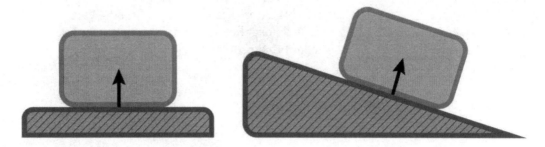

TENSION

Concept: the pulling force from a cord

Another force that may come into play on the exam is called tension. Anytime a cord is attached to a body and pulled so that it is taut, we may say that the cord is under tension. The cord in tension applies a pulling tension force on the connected objects. This force is pointed away from the body and along the cord at the point of attachment. In simple considerations of tension, the cord is assumed to be both without mass and incapable of stretching. In other words, its only role is as the connector between two bodies. The cord is also assumed to pull on both ends with the same magnitude of tension force.

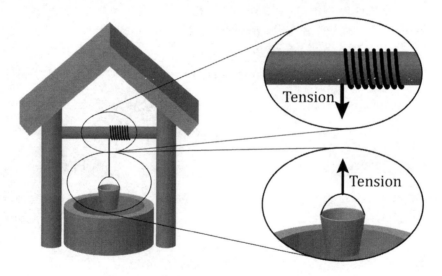

FRICTION

Concept: Friction is a resistance to motion between contacting surfaces

In order to illustrate the concept of friction, let us imagine a book resting on a table. As it sits, the force of its weight is equal to and opposite of the normal force. If, however, we were to exert a force on the book, attempting to push it to one side, a frictional force would arise, equal and opposite to our force. This kind of frictional force is known as static frictional force.

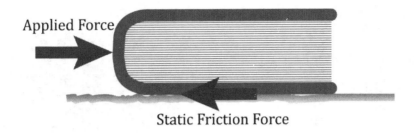

Static Friction Force

As we increase our force on the book, however, we will eventually cause it to accelerate in the direction of our force. At this point, the frictional force opposing us will be known as kinetic friction. For many combinations of surfaces, the magnitude of the kinetic frictional force is lower than that of the static frictional force, and consequently, the amount of force needed to maintain the movement of the book will be less than that needed to initiate the movement.

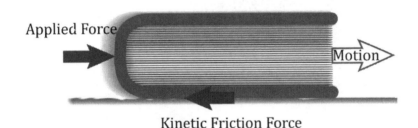

Kinetic Friction Force

ROLLING FRICTION

Occasionally, a question will ask you to consider the amount of friction generated by an object that is rolling. If a wheel is rolling at a constant speed, then the point at which it touches the ground will not slide, and there will be no friction between the ground and the wheel inhibiting movement. In fact, the friction at the point of contact between the wheel and the ground is static friction necessary to propulsion with wheels. When a vehicle accelerates, the static friction between the wheels and ground allows the vehicle to achieve acceleration. Without this friction, the vehicle would spin its wheels and go nowhere.

Although the static friction does not impede movement for the wheels, a combination of frictional forces can resist rolling motion. One such frictional force is bearing friction. Bearing friction is the kinetic friction between the wheel and an object it rotates around, such as a stationary axle.

Most questions will consider bearing friction the only force stopping a rotating wheel. There are many other factors that affect the efficiency of a rolling wheel such as deformation of the wheel, deformation of the surface, and force imbalances, but the net resulting friction can be modeled as a simple kinetic rolling friction. Rolling friction or rolling resistance is the catch-all friction for the combination of all the losses which impede wheels in real life.

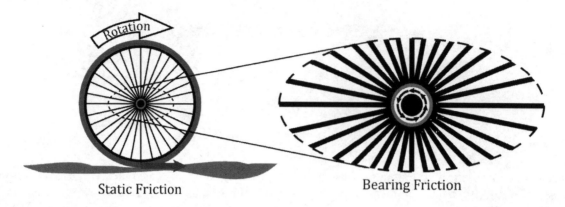

Static Friction   Bearing Friction

DRAG FORCE

Friction can also be generated when an object is moving through air or liquid. A drag force occurs when a body moves through some fluid (either liquid or gas) and experiences a force that opposes the motion of the body. The drag force is greater if the air or fluid is thicker or is moving in the direction opposite to the object. Obviously, the higher the drag force, the greater amount of positive force required to keep the object moving forward.

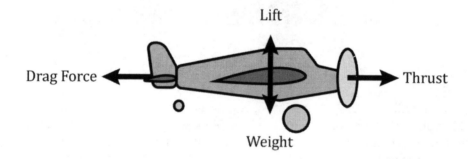

BALANCED FORCES

An object is in equilibrium when the sum of all forces acting on the object is zero. When the forces on an object sum to zero, the object does not accelerate. Equilibrium can be obtained when forces in the y-direction sum to zero, forces in the x-direction sum to zero, or forces in both directions sum to zero.

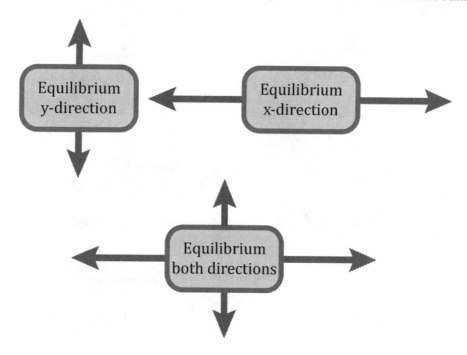

In most cases, a problem will provide one or more forces acting on object and ask for a force to balance the system. The force will be the opposite of the current force or sum of current forces.

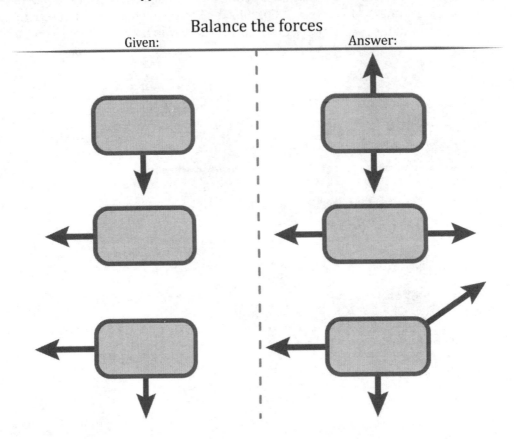

Balance the forces

Given: Answer:

ROTATIONAL KINETICS

Many equations and concepts in linear kinematics and kinetics transfer to rotation. For example, angular position is an angle. Angular velocity, like linear velocity, is the change in the position (angle) divided by the time. Angular acceleration is the change in angular velocity divided by time. Although most tests will not require you to perform angular calculations, they will expect you to understand the angular version of force: torque.

Concept: Torque is a twisting force on an object

Calculation: Torque = radius × force

Torque, like force, is a vector and has magnitude and direction. As with force, the sum of torques on an object will affect the angular acceleration of that object. The key to solving problems with torque is understanding the lever arm. A better description of the torque equation is:

Torque = force × the distance perpedicular to the force to the center of rotation

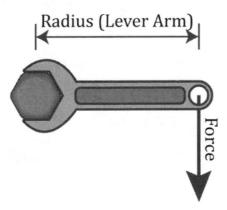

Because torque is directly proportional to the radius, or lever arm, a greater lever arm will result in a greater torque with the same amount of force. The wrench on the right has twice the radius and, as a result, twice the torque.

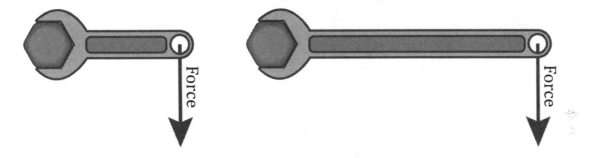

Alternatively, a greater force also increases torque. The wrench on the right has twice the force and twice the torque.

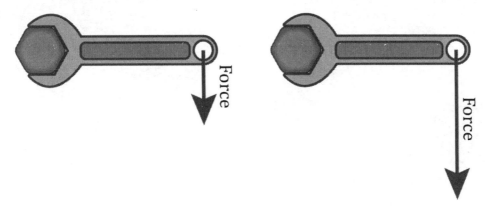

Work/Energy

WORK

Concept: Work is the transfer of energy from one object to another

Calculation: Work = force × displacement

The equation for work in one dimension is fairly simple:

$$\textbf{Work} = \textbf{Force} \times \textbf{displacement}$$

$$\textbf{W} = \textbf{F} \times \textbf{d}$$

In the equation, the force and the displacement are the magnitude of the force exerted and the total change in position of the object on which the force is exerted, respectively. If force and displacement have the same direction, then the work is positive. If they are in opposite directions, however, the work is negative.

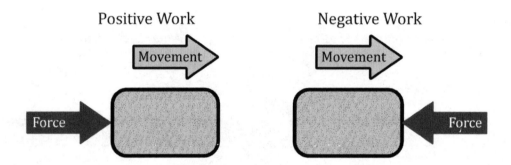

For two-dimensional work, the equation is a bit more complex:

$$\textbf{Work} = \textbf{Force} \times \textbf{displacement} \times \textbf{cos(θ between displacement and force)}$$

$$\textbf{W} = \textbf{F} \times \textbf{d} \times \textbf{cos(θ)}$$

The angle in the equation is the angle between the direction of the force and the direction of the displacement. Thus, the work done when a box is pulled at a 20 degree angle with a force of 100 lb for 20 ft will be less than the work done when a differently weighted box is pulled horizontally with a force of 100 lb for 20 ft.

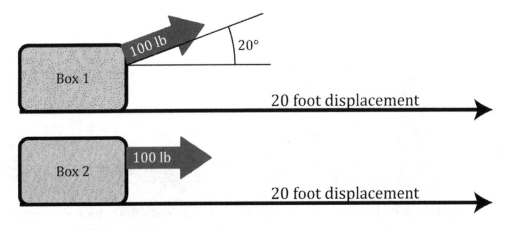

$$W_1 = 100\text{lb} \times 20\text{ft} \times \cos(20°) = 1880 \text{ ft} \cdot \text{lb}$$

$$W_2 = 100\text{lb} \times 20\text{ft} \times \cos(0°) = 2000 \text{ ft} \cdot \text{lb}$$

The unit ft · lb is the unit for both work and energy.

ENERGY

Concept: the ability of a body to do work on another object

Energy is a word that has found a million different uses in the English language, but in physics it refers to the measure of a body's ability to do work. In physics, energy may not have a million meanings, but it does have many forms. Each of these forms, such as chemical, electric, and nuclear, is the capability of an object to perform work. However, for the purpose of most tests, mechanical energy and mechanical work are the only forms of energy worth understanding in depth. Mechanical energy is the sum of an object's kinetic and potential energies. Although they will be introduced in greater detail, these are the forms of mechanical energy:

Kinetic Energy – energy an object has by virtue of its motion

Gravitational Potential Energy – energy by virtue of an object's height

Elastic Potential Energy – energy stored in compression or tension

Neglecting frictional forces, mechanical energy is conserved.

As an example, imagine a ball moving perpendicular to the surface of the earth, with its weight the only force acting on it. As the ball rises, the weight will be doing work on the ball, decreasing its speed and its kinetic energy, and slowing it down until it momentarily stops. During this ascent, the potential energy of the ball will be rising. Once the ball begins to fall back down, it will lose potential energy as it gains kinetic energy. Mechanical energy is conserved throughout; the potential energy of the ball at its highest point is equal to the kinetic energy of the ball at its lowest point prior to impact.

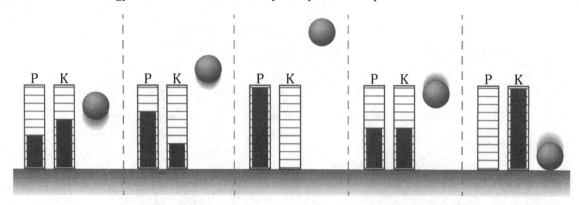

In systems where friction and air resistance are not negligible, we observe a different sort of result. For example, imagine a block sliding across the floor until it comes to a stop due to friction. Unlike a compressed spring or a ball flung into the air, there is no way for this block to regain its energy with a return trip. Therefore, we cannot say that the lost kinetic energy is being stored as potential energy. Instead, it has been dissipated and cannot be recovered. The total mechanical energy of the block-floor system has been not conserved in this case but rather reduced. The total energy of the system has not decreased, since the kinetic energy has been converted into thermal energy, but that energy is no longer useful for work.

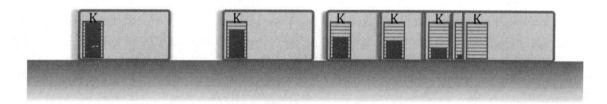

Energy, though it may change form, will be neither created nor destroyed during physical processes. However, if we construct a system and some external force performs work on it, the result may be slightly different. If the work is positive, then the overall store of energy is increased; if it is negative, however, we can say that the overall energy of the system has decreased.

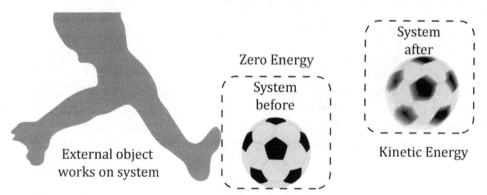

KINETIC ENERGY

The kinetic energy of an object is the amount of energy it possesses by reason of being in motion. Kinetic energy cannot be negative. Changes in kinetic energy will occur when a force does work on an object, such that the motion of the object is altered. This change in kinetic energy is equal to the amount of work that is done. This relationship is commonly referred to as the work-energy theorem.

One interesting application of the work-energy theorem is that of objects in a free fall. To begin with, let us assert that the force acting on such an object is its weight, equal to its mass times g (the force of gravity). The work done by this force will be positive, as the force is exerted in the direction in which the object is traveling. Kinetic energy will, therefore, increase, according to the work-kinetic energy theorem.

If the object is dropped from a great enough height, it eventually reaches its terminal velocity, where the drag force is equal to the weight, so the object is no longer accelerating and its kinetic energy remains constant.

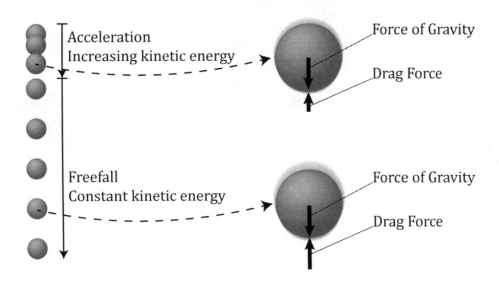

GRAVITATIONAL POTENTIAL ENERGY

Gravitational potential energy is simply the potential for a certain amount of work to be done by one object on another using gravity. For objects on earth, the gravitational potential energy is equal to the amount of work which the earth can act on the object. The work which gravity performs on objects moving entirely or partially in the vertical direction is equal to the force exerted by the earth (weight) times the distance traveled in the direction of the force (height above the ground or reference point):

$$\text{Work from gravity} = \text{weight} \times \text{height above the ground}$$

Thus, the gravitational potential energy is the same as the potential work.

Gravitational Potential Energy = weight × height

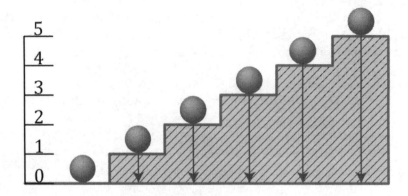

ELASTIC POTENTIAL ENERGY

Elastic potential energy is the potential for a certain amount of work to be done by one object on another using elastic compression or tension. The most common example is the spring. A spring will resist any compression or tension away from its equilibrium position (natural position). A small buggy is pressed into a large spring. The spring contains a large amount of elastic potential energy. If the buggy and spring are released, the spring will push exert a force on the buggy for a distance. This work will put kinetic energy into the buggy. The energy can be imagined as a liquid poured from one container into another. The spring pours its elastic energy into the buggy, which receives the energy as kinetic energy.

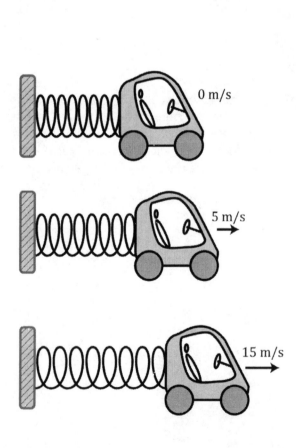

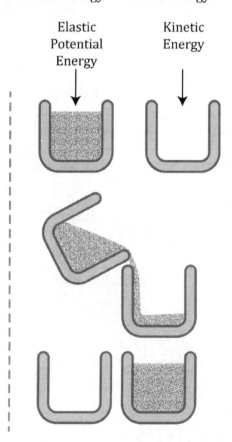

POWER

Concept: the rate of work

Calculation: work/time

On occasion, you may need to demonstrate an understanding of power, as it is defined in applied physics. Power is the rate at which work is done. Power, like work and energy, is a scalar quantity. Power can be calculated by dividing the amount of work performed by the amount of time in which the work was performed.

$$\text{Power} = \frac{\text{work}}{\text{time}}$$

If more work is performed in a shorter amount of time, more power has been exerted. Power can be expressed in a variety of units. The preferred metric expression is one of watts or joules per seconds. For engine power, it is often expressed in horsepower.

Machines

SIMPLE MACHINES

Concept: Tools which transform forces to make tasks easier.

As their job is to transform forces, simple machines have an input force and an output force or forces. Simple machines transform forces in two ways: direction and magnitude. A machine can change the direction of a force, with respect to the input force, like a single stationary pulley which only changes the direction of the output force. A machine can also change the magnitude of the force like a lever.

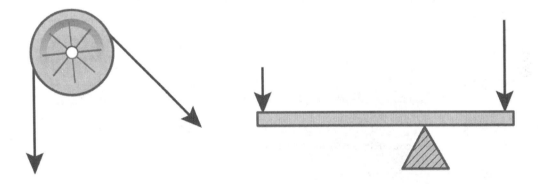

Simple machines include the inclined plane, the wedge, the screw, the pulley, the lever, and the wheel.

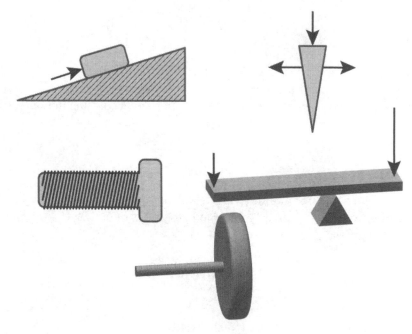

MECHANICAL ADVANTAGE

Concept: the amount of change a simple machine provides to the magnitude of a force

Calculation: output force/input force

Mechanical advantage is the measure of the output force divided by the input force. Thus, mechanical advantage measures the change performed by a machine. Machines cannot create energy, only transform it. Thus, in frictionless, ideal machines, the input work equals the output work.

$$\text{Work}_{input} = \text{Work}_{output}$$

$$\text{force}_{input} \times \text{distance}_{input} = \text{force}_{output} \times \text{distance}_{output}$$

This means that a simple machine can increase the force of the output by decreasing the distance which the output travels or it can increase the distance of the output by decreasing the force at the output.

By moving parts of the equation for work, we can arrive at the equation for mechanical advantage.

$$\text{Mechanical Advantage} = \frac{\text{force}_{output}}{\text{force}_{input}} = \frac{\text{distance}_{input}}{\text{distance}_{output}}$$

If the mechanical advantage is greater than one, the output force is greater than the input force and the input distance is greater than the output distance. Conversely, if the mechanical advantage is less than one, the input force is greater than the output force and the output distance is greater than the input distance. In equation form this is:

If Mechanical Advantage > 1:

$$\text{force}_{input} < \text{force}_{output} \text{ and distance}_{output} < \text{distance}_{input}$$

If Mechanical Advantage < 1:

$$\text{force}_{\text{input}} > \text{force}_{\text{output}} \text{ and } \text{distance}_{\text{output}} > \text{distance}_{\text{input}}$$

INCLINED PLANE

The inclined plane is perhaps the most common of the simple machines. It is simply a flat surface that elevates as you move from one end to the other; a ramp is an easy example of an inclined plane. Consider how much easier it is for an elderly person to walk up a long ramp than to climb a shorter but steeper flight of stairs; this is because the force required is diminished as the distance increases. Indeed, the longer the ramp, the easier it is to ascend.

On the exam, this simple fact will most often be applied to moving heavy objects. For instance, if you have to move a heavy box onto the back of a truck, it is much easier to push it up a ramp than to lift it directly onto the truck bed. The longer the ramp, the greater the mechanical advantage, and the easier it will be to move the box. The mechanical advantage of an inclined plane is equal to the slant length divided by the rise of the plane.

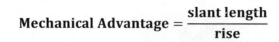

$$\text{Mechanical Advantage} = \frac{\text{slant length}}{\text{rise}}$$

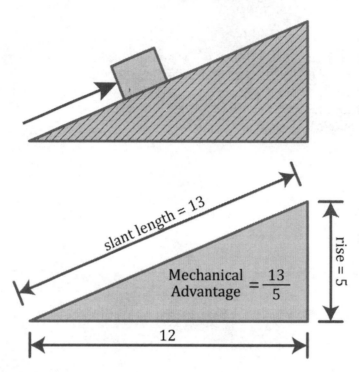

slant length = 13

$$\text{Mechanical Advantage} = \frac{13}{5}$$

rise = 5

12

As you solve this kind of problem, however, remember that the same amount of work is being performed whether the box is lifted directly or pushed up a twenty-foot ramp; a simple machine only changes the force and the distance.

WEDGE

A wedge is a variation on the inclined plane, in which the wedge moves between objects or parts and forces them apart. The unique characteristic of a wedge is that, unlike an inclined plane, it is designed to move. Perhaps the most familiar use of the wedge is in splitting wood. A wedge is driven into the wood by hitting the flat back end. The thin end of a wedge is easier to drive into the wood since it has less surface area and, therefore, transmits more force per area. As the wedge is driven in, the increased width helps to split the wood.

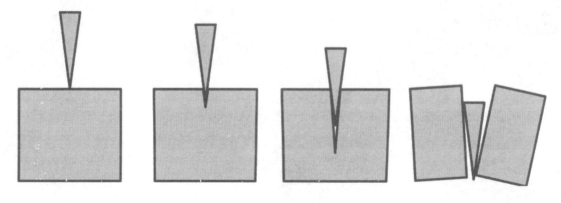

The exam may require you to select the wedge that has the highest mechanical advantage. This should be easy: the longer and thinner the wedge, the greater the mechanical advantage. The equation for mechanical advantage is:

$$\text{Mechanical Advantage} = \frac{\textbf{Length}}{\textbf{Width}}$$

SCREW

A screw is simply an inclined plane that has been wound around a cylinder so that it forms a sort of spiral.

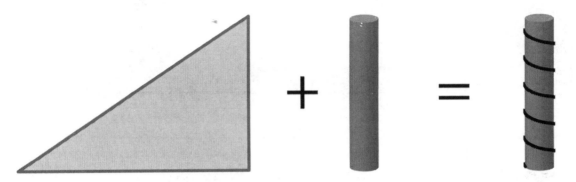

When it is placed into some medium, as for instance wood, the screw will move either forward or backward when it is rotated. The principle of the screw is used in a number of different objects, from jar lids to flashlights. On the exam, you are unlikely to see many questions regarding screws, though you may be presented with a given screw rotation and asked in which direction the screw will move. However, for consistency's sake, the equation for the mechanical advantage is a modification of the inclined plane's equation. Again, the formula for an inclined plane is:

$$\text{Mechanical Advantage} = \frac{\textbf{slant length}}{\textbf{rise}}$$

Because the rise of the inclined plane is the length along a screw, length between rotations = rise. Also, the slant length will equal the circumference of one rotation = 2πr.

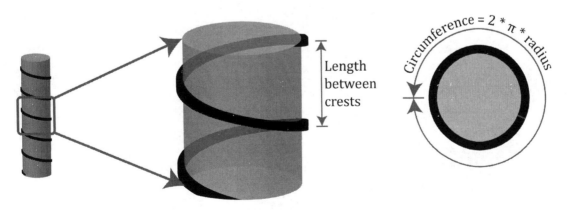

$$\text{Mechanical Advantage} = \frac{\textbf{2} \times \boldsymbol{\pi} \times \textbf{radius}}{\textbf{length between crests}}$$

LEVER

The lever is the most common kind of simple machine. See-saws, shovels, and baseball bats are all examples of levers. There are three classes of levers which are differentiated by the relative orientations of the fulcrum, resistance, and effort. The fulcrum is the point at which the lever rotates; the effort is the point on the lever where force is applied; the resistance is the part of the lever that acts in response to the effort.

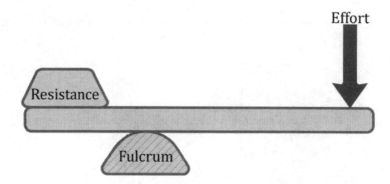

The mechanical advantage of a lever depends on the distances of the effort and resistance from the fulcrum. Mechanical advantage equals:

$$\text{Mechanical Advantage} = \frac{\text{effort distance}}{\text{resistance distance}}$$

For each class of lever, the location of the important distances changes:

First Class Lever

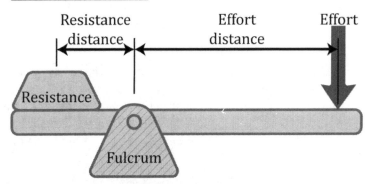

Second Class Lever

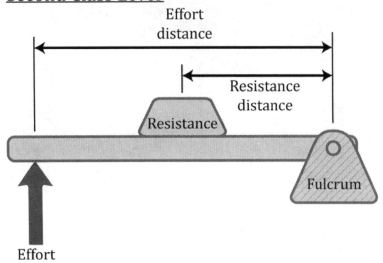

Third Class Lever

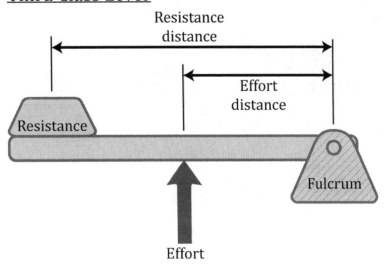

In a first class lever, the fulcrum is between the effort and the resistance. A seesaw is a good example of a first class lever: when effort is applied to force one end up, the other end goes down, and vice versa. The shorter the distance between the fulcrum and the resistance, the easier it will be to move the resistance. As an example, consider whether it is easier to lift another person on a see-saw when they are sitting close to the middle or all the way at the end. A little practice will show you that it is much more difficult to lift a person the farther away he or she is on the see-saw.

In a second class lever, the resistance is in-between the fulcrum and the effort. While a first class lever is able to increase force and distance through mechanical advantage, a second class lever is only able to increase force. A common example of a second class lever is the wheelbarrow: the force exerted by your hand at one end of the wheelbarrow is magnified at the load. Basically, with a second class lever you are trading distance for force; by moving your end of the wheelbarrow a bit farther, you produce greater force at the load.

Third class levers are used to produce greater distance. In a third class lever, the force is applied in between the fulcrum and the resistance. A baseball bat is a classic example of a third class lever; the bottom of the bat, below where you grip it, is considered the fulcrum. The end of the bat, where the ball is struck, is the resistance. By exerting effort at the base of the bat, close to the fulcrum, you are able to make the end of the bat fly quickly through the air. The closer your hands are to the base of the bat, the faster you will be able to make the other end of the bat travel.

PULLEY

The pulley is a simple machine in which a rope is carried by the rotation of a wheel. Another name for a pulley is a block. Pulleys are typically used to allow the force to be directed from a convenient location. For instance, imagine you are given the task of lifting a heavy and tall bookcase. Rather than tying a rope to the bookcase and trying to lift it up, it would make sense to tie a pulley system to a rafter above the bookcase and run the rope through it, so that you could pull down on the rope and lift the bookcase.

Pulling down allows you to incorporate your weight (normal force) into the act of lifting, thereby making it easier.

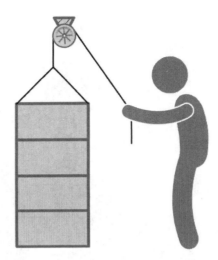

If there is just one pulley above the bookcase, you have created a first-class lever which will not diminish the amount of force that needs to be applied to lift the bookcase. There is another way to use a pulley, however, that can make the job of lifting a heavy object considerably easier. First, tie the rope directly to the rafter. Then, attach a pulley to the top of the bookcase and run the rope through it. If you can then stand so that you are above the bookcase, you will have a much easier time lifting this heavy object. Why? Because the weight of the bookcase is now being distributed: half of it is acting on the rafter, and half of it is acting on you. In other words, this arrangement allows you to lift an object with half the force. This simple pulley system, therefore, has a mechanical advantage of 2. Note that in this arrangement, the unfixed pulley is acting like a second-class lever. The price you pay for your mechanical advantage is that whatever distance you raise your end of the rope, the bookcase will only be lifted half as much.

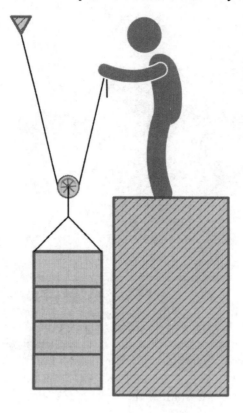

Of course, it might be difficult for you to find a place high enough to enact this system. If this is the case, you can always tie another pulley to the rafter and run the rope through it and back down to the floor. Since this second pulley is fixed, the mechanical advantage will remain the same.

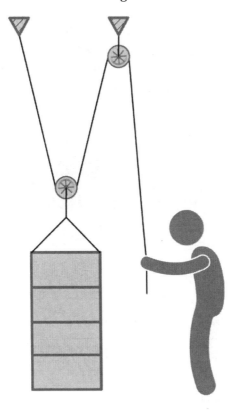

There are other, slightly more complex ways to obtain an even greater mechanical advantage with a system of pulleys. On the exam, you may be required to determine the pulley and tackle (rope) arrangement that creates the greatest mechanical advantage. The easiest way to determine the answer is to count the number of ropes that are going to and from the unfixed pulley; the more ropes coming and going, the greater the mechanical advantage.

WHEEL AND AXLE

Another basic arrangement that makes use of simple machines is called the wheel and axle. When most people think of a wheel and axle, they immediately envision an automobile tire. The steering wheel of the car, however, operates on the same mechanical principle, namely that the force required to move the center of a circle is much greater than the force require to move the outer rim of a circle. When you turn the steering wheel, you are essentially using a second-class lever by increasing the output force by increasing the input distance. The force required to turn the wheel from the outer rim is much less than would be required to turn the wheel from its center. Just imagine how difficult it would be to drive a car if the steering wheel was the size of a saucer!

Conceptually, the mechanical advantage of a wheel is easy to understand. For instance, all other things being equal, the mechanical advantage created by a system will increase along with the radius. In other words, a steering wheel with a radius of 12 inches has a greater mechanical advantage than a steering wheel with a radius of ten inches; the same amount of force exerted on the rim of each wheel will produce greater force at the axis of the larger wheel.

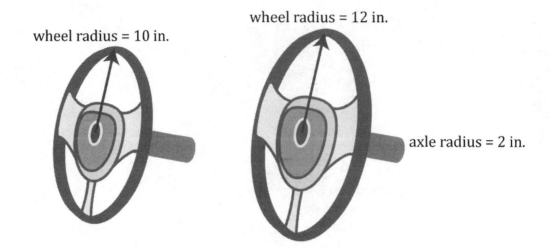

The equation for the mechanical advantage of a wheel and axle is:

$$\textbf{Mechanical Advantage} = \frac{\textbf{radius}_{\textbf{wheel}}}{\textbf{radius}_{\textbf{axle}}}$$

Thus, the mechanical advantage of the steering wheel with a larger radius will be:

$$\text{Mechanical Advantage} = \frac{12 \text{ inches}}{2 \text{ inches}} = 6$$

GEARS

The exam may ask you questions involving some slightly more complex mechanisms. It is very common, for instance, for there to be a couple of questions concerning gears. Gears are a system of interlocking wheels that can create immense mechanical advantages. The amount of mechanical advantage, however, will depend on the gear ratio; that is, on the relation in size between the gears.

When a small gear is driving a big gear, the speed of the big gear is relatively slow; when a big gear is driving a small gear, the speed of the small gear is relatively fast.

The equation for the mechanical advantage is:

$$\text{Mechanical Advantage} = \frac{\text{Torque}_{\text{output}}}{\text{Torque}_{\text{input}}} = \frac{r_{\text{output}}}{r_{\text{input}}} = \frac{\#\ \text{of teeth}_{\text{output}}}{\#\ \text{of teeth}_{\text{input}}}$$

Note that mechanical advantage is greater than 1 when the output gear is larger. In these cases, the output velocity (ω) will be lower. The equation for the relative speed of a gear system is:

$$\frac{\omega_{\text{input}}}{\omega_{\text{output}}} = \frac{r_{\text{output}}}{r_{\text{input}}}$$

$$\text{Mechanical Advantage} = \frac{\text{teeth}_{\text{output}}}{\text{teeth}_{\text{input}}} = \frac{20}{10} = 2$$

$$\text{Mechanical Advantage} = \frac{\text{teeth}_{\text{output}}}{\text{teeth}_{\text{input}}} = \frac{16}{8} = 2$$

USES OF GEARS

Gears are used to change direction of output torque, change location of output torque, change amount of output torque, and change angular velocity of output.

Change output direction

Change torque location

Change torque amount

Change output velocity

GEAR RATIOS

A gear ratio is a measure of how much the speed and torque are changing in a gear system. It is the ratio of output speed to input speed. Because the number of teeth is directly proportional to the speed in meshing gears, a gear ratio can also be calculated using the number of teeth on the gears. When the driving gear has 30 teeth and the driven gear has 10 teeth, the gear ratio is 3:1.

$$\text{Gear Ratio} = \frac{\text{\# of teeth}_{\text{driving}}}{\text{\# of teeth}_{\text{driven}}} = \frac{30}{10} = \frac{3}{1} = 3:1$$

This means that the smaller, driven gear rotates 3 times for every 1 rotation of the driving gear.

72

THE HYDRAULIC JACK

The hydraulic jack is a simple machine using two tanks and two pistons to change the amount of an output force.

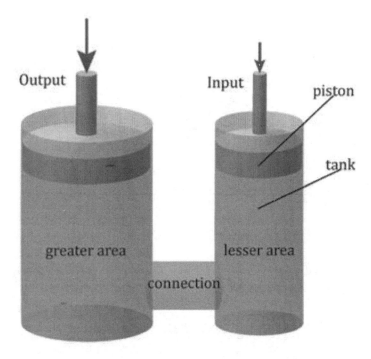

Since fluids are effectively incompressible, when you apply pressure to one part of a contained fluid, that pressure will have to be relieved in equal measure elsewhere in the container. Supposed the input piston has half the surface area of the output piston (10 in² compared to 20 in²), and it is being pushed downward with 50 pounds of force. The pressure being applied to the fluid is $50\ lb \div 10\ in^2 = 5\frac{lb}{in^2}$ or 5 psi. When that 5 psi of pressure is applied to the output piston, it pushes that piston upward with a force of $5\frac{lb}{in^2} \times 20\ in^2 = 100\ lb$.

The hydraulic jack functions similarly to a first class lever, but with the important factor being the area of the pistons rather than the length of the lever arms. Note that the mechanical advantage is based on the relative areas, not the relative radii, of the pistons. The radii must be squared to compute the relative areas.

$$\textbf{Mechanical Advantage} = \frac{\textbf{Force}_{\textbf{output}}}{\textbf{Force}_{\textbf{input}}} = \frac{\textbf{area}_{\textbf{output}}}{\textbf{area}_{\textbf{input}}} = \frac{\textbf{radius}_{\textbf{output}}^{2}}{\textbf{radius}_{\textbf{input}}^{2}}$$

PULLEYS AND BELTS

Another system involves two pulleys connected by a drive belt (a looped band that goes around both pulleys). The operation of this system is similar to that of gears, with the exception that the pulleys will rotate in the same direction, while interlocking gears will rotate in opposite directions. A smaller pulley will always spin faster than a larger pulley, though the larger pulley will generate more torque.

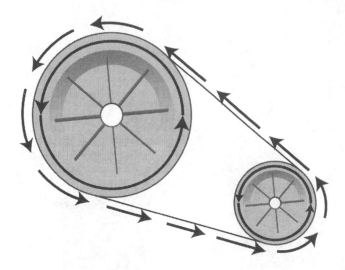

The speed ratio between the pulleys can be determined by comparing their radii; for instance, a 4-inch pulley and a 12-inch pulley will have a speed ratio of 3:1.

Momentum/Impulse

LINEAR MOMENTUM

Concept: how much a body will resist stopping

Calculation: $momentum = mass \times velocity$

In physics, linear momentum can be found by multiplying the mass and velocity of an object:

$$\textbf{Momentum} = \textbf{mass} \times \textbf{velocity}$$

Momentum and velocity will always be in the same direction. Newton's second law describes momentum, stating that the rate of change of momentum is proportional to the force exerted and is in the direction of the force. If we assume a closed and isolated system (one in which no objects leave or enter, and upon which the sum of external forces is zero), then we can assume that the momentum of the system will neither increase nor decrease. That is, we will find that the momentum is a constant. The law of conservation of linear momentum applies universally in physics, even in situations of extremely high velocity or with subatomic particles.

COLLISIONS

This concept of momentum takes on new importance when we consider collisions. A collision is an isolated event in which a strong force acts between each of two or more colliding bodies for a brief period of time. However, a collision is more intuitively defined as one or more objects hitting each other.

When two bodies collide, each object exerts a force on the opposite member. These equal and opposite forces change the linear momentum of the objects. However, when both bodies are considered, the net momentum in collisions is conserved.

There are two types of collisions: elastic and inelastic. The difference between the two lies in whether kinetic energy is conserved. If the total kinetic energy of the system is conserved, the collision is elastic. Visually, elastic collisions are collisions in which objects bounce perfectly. If some of the kinetic energy is transformed into heat or another form of energy, the collision is inelastic. Visually, inelastic collisions are collisions in which the objects do not bounce perfectly or even stick to each other.

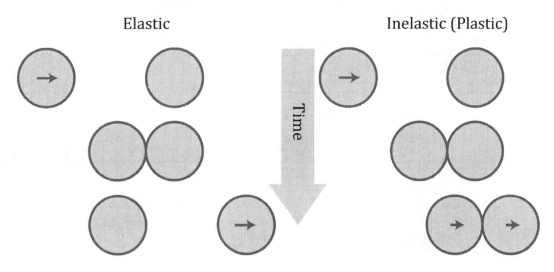

If the two bodies involved in an elastic collision have the same mass, then the body that was moving will stop completely, and the body that was at rest will begin moving at the same velocity as the projectile was moving before the collision.

Fluids

FLUIDS

Concept: liquids and gasses

A few of the questions on the exam will probably require you to consider the behavior of fluids. It sounds obvious, perhaps, but fluids can best be defined as substances that flow. A fluid will conform, slowly or quickly, to any container in which it is placed. Both liquids and gasses are considered to be fluids. Fluids are essentially those substances in which the atoms are not arranged in any permanent, rigid way. In ice, for instance, atoms are all lined up in what is known as a crystalline lattice, while in water and steam the only intermolecular arrangements are haphazard connections between neighboring molecules.

FLOW RATES

When liquids flow in and out of containers with certain rates, the change in volume is the volumetric flow in minus the volumetric flow out. Volumetric flow is essentially the amount of volume moved past some point divided by the time it took for the volume to pass.

$$\text{Volumetric flow rate} = \frac{\text{volume moved}}{\text{time for the movement}}$$

If the flow into a container is greater than the flow out, the container will fill with the fluid. However, if the flow out of a container is greater than the flow into a container, the container will drain of the fluid.

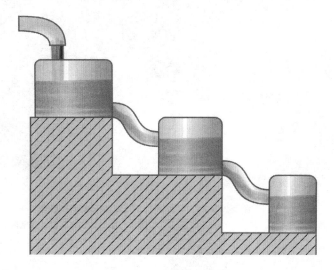

DENSITY

Concept: How much mass is in a specific volume of a Substance

Calculation: density $= \rho = \frac{\text{mass}}{\text{volume}}$

Density is essentially how much stuff there is in a volume or space. The density of a fluid is generally expressed with the symbol ρ (the Greek letter rho.) The density may be found with the simple equation:

$$\text{density} = \rho = \frac{\text{mass}}{\text{volume}}$$

Density is a scalar property, meaning that it has no direction component.

PRESSURE

Concept: The amount of force applied per area

Calculation: Pressure $= \frac{\text{force}}{\text{area}}$

Pressure, like fluid density, is a scalar and does not have a direction. The equation for pressure is concerned only with the magnitude of that force, not with the direction in which it is pointing. The SI unit of pressure is the Newton per square meter, or Pascal.

$$\text{Pressure} = \frac{\text{force}}{\text{area}}$$

As every deep-sea diver knows, the pressure of water becomes greater the deeper you go below the surface; conversely, experienced mountain climbers know that air pressure decreases as they gain a higher altitude. These pressures are typically referred to as hydrostatic pressures because they involve fluids at rest.

Pascal's Principle

The exam may also require you to demonstrate some knowledge of how fluids move. Anytime you squeeze a tube of toothpaste, you are demonstrating the idea known as Pascal's principle. This principle states that a change in the pressure applied to an enclosed fluid is transmitted undiminished to every portion of the fluid as well as to the walls of the containing vessel.

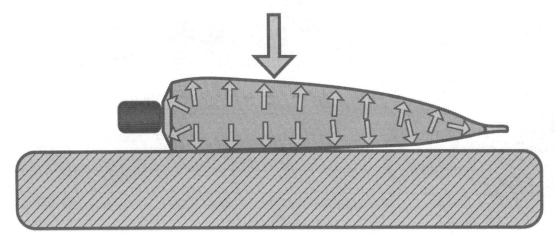

Buoyant Force

If an object is submerged in water, it will have a buoyant force exerted on it in the upward direction. Often, of course, this buoyant force is much too small to keep an object from sinking to the bottom.

Buoyancy is summarized in Archimedes' principle; a body wholly or partially submerged in a fluid will be buoyed up by a force equal to the weight of the fluid that the body displaces.

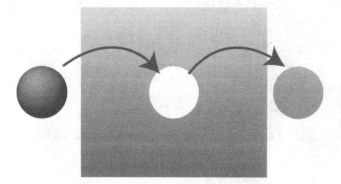 

If the buoyant force is greater than the weight of an object, the object will go upward. If the weight of the object is greater than the buoyant force, the object will sink. When an object is floating on the surface, the buoyant force has the same magnitude as the weight.

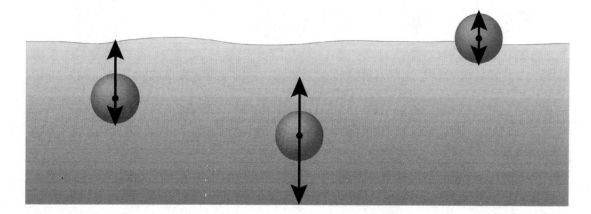

Even though the weight of a floating object is precisely balanced by a buoyant force, these forces will not necessarily act at the same point. The weight will act from the center of mass of the object, while the buoyancy will act from the center of mass of the hole in the water made by the object (known as the center of buoyancy). If the floating object is tilted, then the center of buoyancy will shift and the object may be unstable. In order to remain in equilibrium, the center of buoyancy must always shift in such a way that the buoyant force and weight provide a restoring torque, one that will restore the body to its upright position. This concept is, of course, crucial to the construction of boats which must always be made to encourage restoring torque.

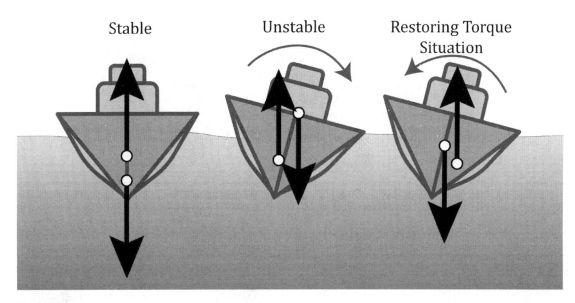

IDEAL FLUIDS

Because the motion of actual fluids is extremely complex, the exam usually assumes ideal fluids when they set up their problems. Using ideal fluids in fluid dynamics problems is like discounting friction in other problems. Therefore, when we deal with ideal fluids, we are making four assumptions. It is important to keep these in mind when considering the behavior of fluids on the exam. First, we are assuming that the flow is steady; in other words, the velocity of every part of the fluid is the same. Second, we assume that fluids are incompressible, and, therefore, have a consistent density. Third, we assume that fluids are nonviscous, meaning that they flow easily and without resistance. Fourth, we assume that the flow of ideal fluids is irrotational: that is, particles in the fluid will not rotate around a center of mass.

BERNOULLI'S PRINCIPLE

When fluids move, they do not create or destroy energy; this modification of Newton's second law for fluid behavior is called Bernoulli's principle. It is essentially just a reformulation of the law of conservation of mechanical energy for fluid mechanics.

The most common application of Bernoulli's principle is that pressure and speed are inversely related, assuming constant altitude. Thus if the elevation of the fluid remains constant and the speed of a fluid particle increases as it travels along a streamline, the pressure will decrease. If the fluid slows down, the pressure will increase.

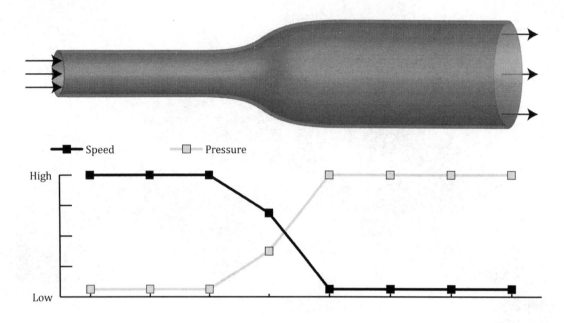

Heat Transfer

HEAT TRANSFER

Heat is a type of energy. Heat transfers from the hot object to the cold object through the three forms of heat transfer: conduction, convection, and radiation.

| Conduction | Convection | Radiation |

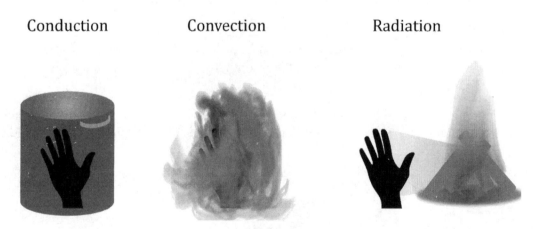

Conduction is the transfer of heat by physical contact. When you touch a hot pot, the pot transfers heat to your hand by conduction.

Convection is the transfer of heat by the movement of fluids. When you put your hand in steam, the steam transfers heat to your hand by convection.

Radiation is the transfer of heat by electromagnetic waves. When you put your hand near a campfire, the fire heats your hand by radiation.

PHASE CHANGES

Materials exist in four phases or states: solid, liquid, gas, and plasma. However, as most tests will not cover plasma, we will focus on solids, liquids, and gases. The solid state is the densest in almost all cases (water is the most notable exception), followed by liquid, and then gas.

The impetus for phase change (changing from one phase to another) is heat. When a solid is heated, it will change into a liquid. The same process of heating will change a liquid into a gas.

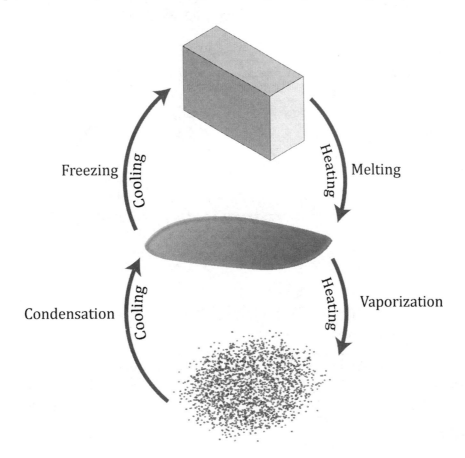

Optics

OPTICS

Lenses change the way light travels. Lenses are able to achieve this by the way in which light travels at different speeds in different mediums. The essentials to optics with lenses deal with concave and convex lenses. Concave lenses make objects appear smaller, while convex lenses make objects appear larger.

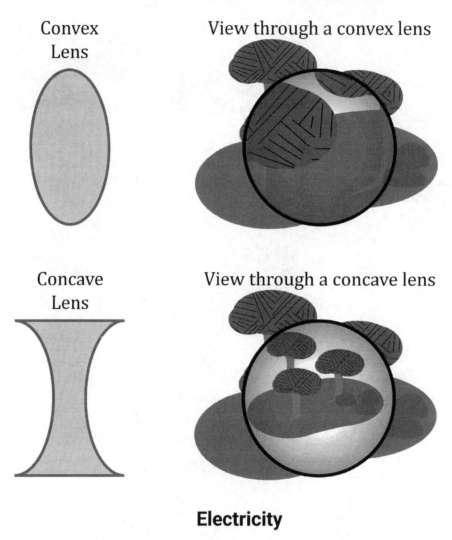

Convex Lens

View through a convex lens

Concave Lens

View through a concave lens

Electricity

ELECTRIC CHARGE

Much like gravity, electricity is an everyday observable phenomenon which is very complex, but may be understood as a set of behaviors. As the gravitational force exists between objects with mass, the electric force exists between objects with electrical charge. In all atoms, the protons have a positive charge, while the electrons have a negative charge. An imbalance of electrons and protons in an object results in a net charge. Unlike gravity, which only pulls, electrical forces can push objects apart as well as pulling them together.

Similar electric charges repel each other. Opposite charges attract each other.

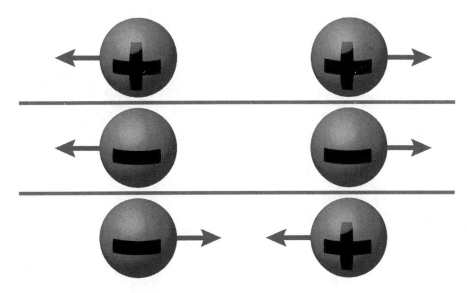

CURRENT

Electrons (and electrical charge with it) move through conductive materials by switching quickly from one atom to another. This electrical flow can manipulate energy like mechanical systems.

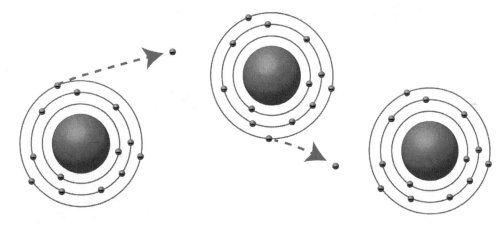

The term for the rate at which the charge flows through a conductive material is current. Because each electron carries a specific charge, current can be thought of as the number of electrons passing a point in a length of time. Current is measured in Amperes (A), each unit of which is approximately 6.24×10^{18} electrons per second.

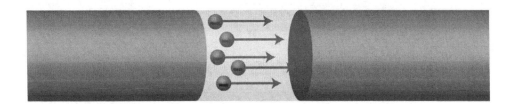

Electric current carries energy much like moving balls carry energy.

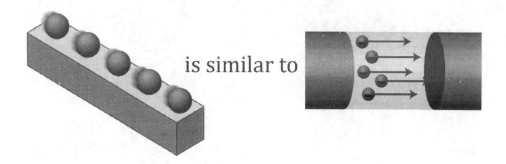

VOLTAGE

Voltage is the potential for electric work. Voltage is the push behind electrical work. Voltage is similar to gravitational potential energy.

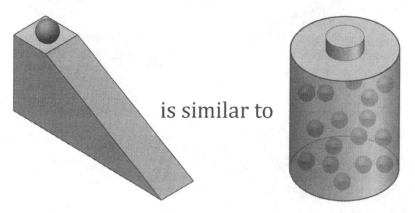

Anything used to generate a voltage, such as a battery or a generator, is called a voltage source. Voltage is conveniently measured in Volts (V).

RESISTANCE

Resistance is the amount of pressure to slow electrical current. Electrical resistance is much like friction, resisting flow and dissipating energy.

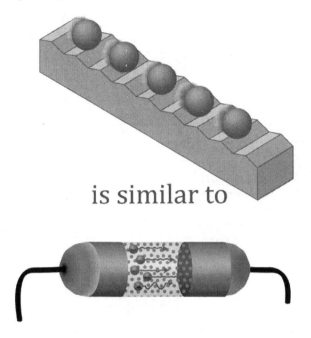

is similar to

Different objects have different resistances. A resistor is an electrical component designed to have a specific resistance, measured in Ohms (Ω).

BASIC CIRCUITS

A circuit is a closed loop through which current can flow. A simple circuit contains a voltage source and a resistor. The current flows from the positive side of the voltage source through the resistor to the negative side of the voltage source.

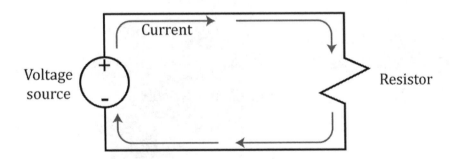

85

If we plot the voltage of a simple circuit, the similarities to gravitational potential energy appear.

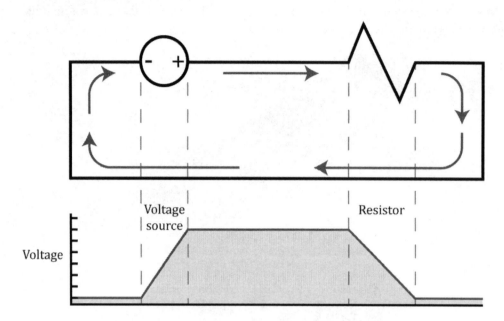

If we consider the circuit to be a track, the electrons would be balls, the voltage source would be a powered lift, and the resistor would be a sticky section of the track. The lift raises the balls, increasing their potential energy. This potential energy is expended as the balls roll down the sticky section of the track.

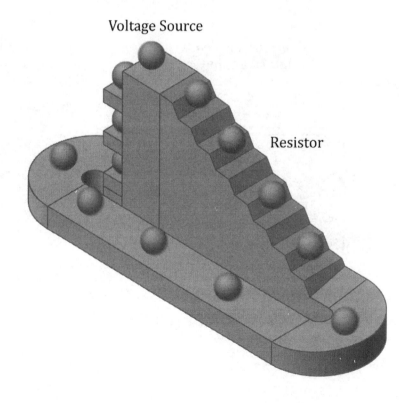

OHM'S LAW

A principle called Ohm's Law explains the relationship between the voltage, current, and resistance. The voltage drop over a resistance is equal to the amount of current times the resistance:

$$\textbf{Voltage (V) = current (I)} \times \textbf{resistance (R)}$$

We can gain a better understanding of this equation by looking at a reference simple circuit and then changing one variable at a time to examine the results.

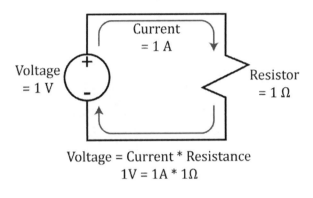

Voltage = Current * Resistance
1V = 1A * 1Ω

Increased Resistance   **Increased Current**   **Increased Voltage**

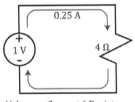 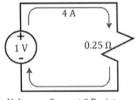 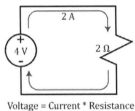

Voltage = Current * Resistance   Voltage = Current * Resistance   Voltage = Current * Resistance
1V = 0.25A * 4Ω   1V = 4A * 0.25Ω   4V = 2A * 2Ω

SERIES CIRCUITS

A series circuit is a circuit with two or more resistors on the same path. The same current runs through both resistors. However, the total voltage drop splits between the resistors. The resistors in series can be added together to make an equivalent basic circuit.

$$R_{equiv} = R_1 + R_2$$

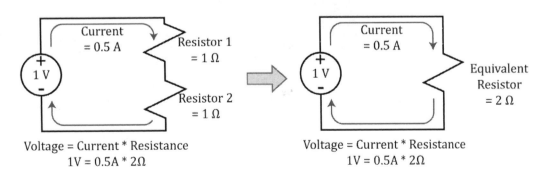

Voltage = Current * Resistance   Voltage = Current * Resistance
1V = 0.5A * 2Ω   1V = 0.5A * 2Ω

PARALLEL CIRCUITS

A parallel circuit is a circuit with two or more resistors on different, parallel paths. Unlike the series circuit, the current splits between the different paths in a parallel circuit. Resistors in parallel can be reduced to an equivalent circuit, but not by simply adding the resistances. The inverse of the equivalent resistance of parallel resistors is equal to the sum of the inverses of the resistance of each leg of the parallel circuit. In equation form that means:

$$\frac{1}{R_{equiv}} = \frac{1}{R_1} + \frac{1}{R_2}$$

Or when solved for equivalent resistance:

$$R_{equiv} = \frac{1}{\frac{1}{R_1} + \frac{1}{R_2}}$$

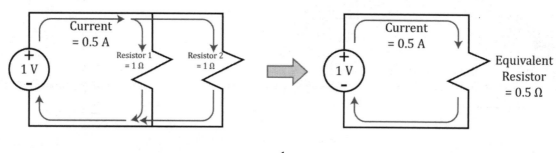

$$R_{equiv} = \frac{1}{\frac{1}{1\,\Omega} + \frac{1}{1\,\Omega}} = 0.5\,\Omega$$

ELECTRICAL POWER

Electrical power, or the energy output over time, is equal to the current resulting from a voltage source times the voltage of that source:

$$\textbf{Power(P)} = \textbf{current (I)} \times \textbf{voltage (V)}$$

Thanks to Ohm's Law, we can write this relation in two other ways:

$$P = I^2 R$$

$$P = \frac{V^2}{R}$$

For instance, if a circuit is composed of a 9 Volt battery and a 3 Ohm resistor, the power output of the battery will be:

$$Power = \frac{V^2}{R} = \frac{9^2}{3} = 27\ Watts$$

AC vs. DC

Up until this point, current has been assumed to flow in one direction. One directional flow is called Direct Current (DC). However, there is another type of electric current: Alternating Current (AC). Many circuits use AC power sources, in which the current flips back and forth rapidly between directions.

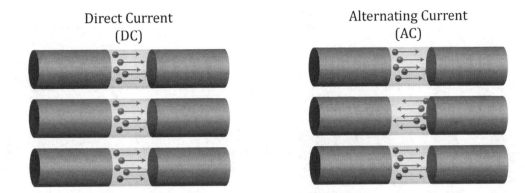

Direct Current (DC)　　　Alternating Current (AC)

CAPACITORS

Capacitors are electrical components which store voltage. Capacitors are made from two conductive surfaces separated from each other by a space and/or insulation. Capacitors resist changes to voltage. Capacitors don't stop AC circuits (although they do affect the current flow), but they do stop DC circuits, acting as open circuits.

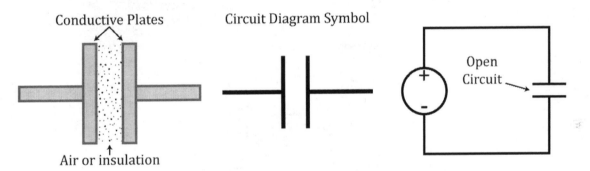

Conductive Plates　　　Circuit Diagram Symbol

Air or insulation

INDUCTORS

Inductors are electrical components which effectively store current. Inductors use the relationship between electricity and magnetism to resist changes in current by running the current through coils of wire. Inductors don't stop DC circuits, but they do resist AC circuits as AC circuits utilize changing currents.

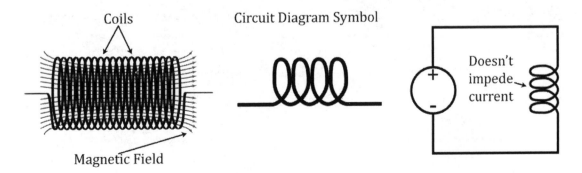

Coils　　　Circuit Diagram Symbol

Magnetic Field

DIODES

Diodes are electrical components which limit the flow of electricity to one direction. If current flows through a diode in the intended direction, the diode will allow the flow. However, a diode will stop current if it runs the wrong way.

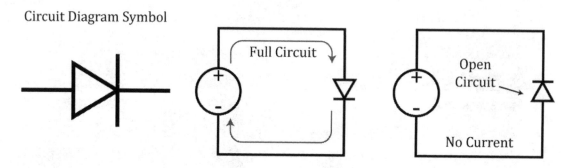

Circuit Diagram Symbol

Full Circuit

Open Circuit

No Current

Magnetism

MAGNETISM

Magnetism is an attraction between opposite poles of magnetic materials and a repulsion between similar poles of magnetic materials. Magnetism can be natural or induced with the use of electric currents. Magnets almost always exist with two polar sides: north and south. A magnetic force exists between two poles on objects. Different poles attract each other. Like poles repel each other.

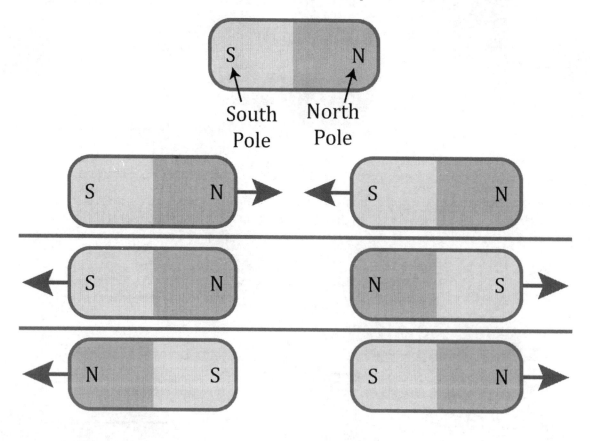

South Pole   North Pole

Aviation and Nautical Information Test

Aviation and Nautical Information Test (ANIT) is only available in computer format; there is no pencil or paper version. It's adaptive, so expect to see at least 20 questions, but no more than 30. The time limit is 15 minutes.

What Are These Questions Testing?

Just as the name of this subtest implies, the aviation and nautical information section tests your knowledge of basic aviation and nautical information, vocabulary, and operations. This includes a wide variety of things including terminology and procedures in both areas, the basic physics involved in flight, aviation history, knowledge of flight deck crew and operations, etc. Unlike the other subtests on the ASTB, this section is essentially a pure test of knowledge, and doesn't test for aptitude at all. Because of this, it's extremely important to prep well for the ANIT section, as it offers the most potential for improving your score since it's all about how much you know about the subjects, and not your innate potential to learn them.

How Can I Improve My Ability to Answer These Questions?

Since these are all knowledge based questions, you can improve your success rate here by reading up on aircraft and nautical information. The section below is an overview of the basics in these areas.

Fixed-wing Aircraft

There are six basic components of a fixed-wing aircraft: wings; fuselage; tail assembly; landing gear; powerplant; and flight controls and control surfaces.

Wings

The **wings** are the primary airfoils of the plane. An airfoil is anything designed to produce lift when it moves through the air. The leading edge of an airfoil is thicker and rounder than the trailing edge, and the top surface of the airfoil has a greater curve than the bottom. The result is that air flows more quickly over the top of the wing, and the greater air pressure beneath pushes the wing, and thus the plane, upwards.

The wings connect to either side of the fuselage. Planes are designated as high-, mid-, and low-wing, depending on where the wings are attached. The wings themselves are described as either cantilever or semi-cantilever. A cantilever wing has sufficient internal support structures to keep it steady in its location. A semi-cantilever wing, on the other hand, requires additional external support structures. The trailing edge of a wing typically has two control surfaces attached by means of a hinge: flaps run from the fuselage to the middle of the wing, and ailerons run from the middle of the wing to the tip. By raising and lowering the flaps and ailerons, the pilot can roll the plane. The plane will roll when the ailerons and flaps are pointed in opposite directions. When the plane is cruising, however, these control surfaces are aligned with the rest of the wing. During takeoff and landing, both surfaces are extended, which increases the lift.

The distance from one wingtip to the other is the wingspan, and the distance from the leading edge to the trailing edge is called the chord. The chord line runs through the wing from leading edge to trailing edge: it divides the wing into upper and lower surfaces. The mean camber line runs along the inside of the wing, such that the parts of the wing above and below it are equal in thickness. The camber is the curvature of the airfoil: if an airfoil is heavily curved, it has a high camber. The thickness of a wing is measured at its greatest point. The shape of the wings when viewed from overhead is known as the planform.

When the wings are not attached parallel to the horizontal plane, the angle they make with the horizontal plane is called the dihedral angle. A positive dihedral wing angle (wings angling above the horizontal plane) keeps the plane stable when it rolls, as it will encourage the plane to return to its original position. This does diminish the maneuverability of the plane, which is why the wings of fighter jets are usually horizontal or even pointed slightly downwards (anhedral).

The shape of the wings has a major influence on the handling, maneuverability, and speed of the plane. Today's planes generally have a straight, sweep, or delta shape. Straight wings may be rectangular, elliptical (rounded), or tapered. They are commonly found on sailplanes, gliders, and other low-speed aircraft.

A swept wing provides better handling at high speeds, but makes the plane slightly less stable at low speeds. Since most modern aircraft are designed to operate at high speeds, this is the most commonly used wing style. Wings may be swept forward or back, though forward-swept wings are rarely seen. In general, a higher angle of sweep is used for planes that are meant to travel faster and be more maneuverable; however, more extreme sweeps require much greater speeds for takeoff and landing.

The delta wing shape is triangular, so that the leading edge of the wing has a high sweep angle while the trailing edge is mostly, if not completely, straight. A delta shape enables the plane to travel but also requires very high takeoff and landing speeds. Many of the earliest supersonic aircraft used the delta wing shape, as did the space shuttles.

FUSELAGE

The **fuselage** is the main body of the airplane. The basic features of the fuselage are the cockpit, cabin, cargo area, and attachment points for external components, like the wings and landing gear. Some planes designed for specific purposes may not have all of these components; for instance, a fighter jet will not have a cabin for passengers or a cargo area, since it needs to be light and maneuverable. The fuselage may be described as either truss or monocoque, depending on whether its strength is created by triangular arrangements of steel or aluminum tubing or by bulkheads, stringers and formers. A stringer is a support structure that runs the length of the fuselage, while a former runs perpendicular.

TAIL ASSEMBLY

The **tail assembly**, or empennage, includes the vertical and horizontal stabilizers, elevators, rudders, and trim tabs. The stabilizers are fixed (non-adjustable) surfaces that extend from the back end of the fuselage. The elevators are positioned along the trailing edges of the horizontal stabilizers; the pilot can move them to raise or lower the nose of the plane. The rudders are connected to the trailing edge of the vertical stabilizer, and are used to move the nose of the plane to the left or right, typically in combination with the ailerons. The trim tabs, finally, are movable surfaces that extend off the trailing edges of the rudder, elevators, and ailerons, and are used to make smaller adjustments.

LANDING GEAR

The **landing gear** usually consists of three sets of wheels used for takeoffs and landings, though some planes have special non-wheel landing gear for landing on snow or water. Landing gear is commonly retractable, meaning that it is pulled up inside the plane during flight to reduce drag. In a typical arrangement, wheel sets are positioned either under each wing or on the sides of the fuselage, with the third wheel set being under the nose or the tail. Having the third wheel set under the nose, known as **tricycle** arrangement, is the most common arrangement on modern aircraft, but having the third wheel set under the tail is still known as **conventional** arrangement. Whether located under the tail or the nose, the third wheel will typically be able to rotate so that the plane can turn while traveling on the ground. The addition of extra wheels to each set allows the plane to handle a greater weight.

POWERPLANT

In aviation, the **powerplant** is the part of the plane that supplies the thrust. A jet engine operates by compressing the air that comes in the front, burning it along with fuel, and then blasting it out the back. There are different methods for compressing the air, but most jet engines do so by slowing it down with a set of small rotating blades. This greatly increases the air pressure at the front of the engine. The compressed air is then forced into a different section, where it is mixed with fuel and burned. As it then expands, it is pushed at great force through a series of turbines, the turning of which moves the compressor blades at the front of the engine, supplying both power and air. The exhausted air then passes out the back of the engine, which propels the plane forward. Some jet engines have afterburners, which feed extra fuel into the area between the turbines and the rear exhaust, increasing forward thrust.

In a propeller plane, on the other hand, the powerplant is the propellers and the engine. The propellers have tilted blades, which push air backwards and thereby push the plane forward. There are two types of propeller: fixed-pitch or variable-pitch. The blade angle of a fixed-pitch propeller cannot be adjusted by the pilot. Variable-pitch propellers allow the pilot, usually indirectly via the plane's control systems, to adjust the pitch of the propeller blades to alter the amount of thrust being generated. Some variable-pitch propellers are designed to operate only at a single rotational speed, allowing the engine to be much simpler and more efficient, so the amount of thrust is controlled entirely by the pitch of the blades. These are known as constant-speed propellers.

The engines of a propeller plane turn the crankshafts, which turn the propellers. The engines also are responsible for powering the plane's electrical system. The location of the engines on a propeller plane may vary. Single-engine planes typically have their engines in front of the fuselage, while multi-engine planes usually have their engines underneath the wings. Some multi-engine planes have engines in both locations.

Flight Envelope

During flight, there are four forces a pilot must manage: lift, gravity, thrust, and drag. These forces act downward (gravity), upward (lift), forward (thrust), and backward (drag). The collective input of these forces is known as the flight envelope.

GRAVITY

The weight of a plane is the primary force that must be overcome for flight to take place. The force of **gravity** on a given object is the same, regardless of orientation, though it varies slightly with large changes in altitude.

Aviation experts distinguish between different types of weight. The basic weight includes the aircraft and any internal or external equipment that will remain a part of the plane during flight. The operating weight is the basic weight plus the crew and any other nonexpendable items not included in the basic weight. The gross weight is the total weight of the aircraft and all contents at any given time. The weight of the airplane when it has no usable fuel is called the zero fuel weight.

LIFT

In order to overcome gravity, the plane must generate **lift**. Lift is the upward force of air pressure on the aircraft, primarily the wings, that allows it to achieve and maintain altitude. In order to generate lift, the plane typically must be traveling forward at considerable speed.

If the wing tilts too far back the airflow may stop over the wing's upper surface, which will result in a rapid loss of altitude and often control of the plane. This is known as a stall, and it may be avoided by decreasing the angle of attack, so that normal airflow over the top of the wing is not interrupted.

THRUST

The speed required for generating lift is provided by the aircraft's **thrust**. It ensures that the aircraft is able to continue moving forward at sufficient speed to generate lift. As was discussed in the previous section, thrust is generated by the powerplant of the aircraft, usually one or more jet engines or propellers.

DRAG

An aircraft's thrust is countered by **drag**, the resistance to forward movement provided by the air that the aircraft is traveling through. At anything above normal walking or running speeds, air resistance is a noticeable hindrance to motion, and it only increases as airspeed goes up. The primary implication that this has on aircraft is that the faster the aircraft goes, the more thrust is required just to overcome the drag and maintain a constant speed.

There are two types of drag: profile drag and induced drag. Profile drag is the drag that exists when any object moves through the air. It is the result of the plane pushing air aside as it moves. Profile drag can be minimized by designing the aircraft to have a better wind profile. Induced drag, on the other hand, is drag that results from the wings generating lift. Part of the process of generating lift involves the wings redirecting the oncoming air downward (think Newton's third law), and this causes additional drag.

ATMOSPHERIC CONDITIONS

The flight envelope is significantly affected by the atmospheric conditions, primarily the density of the surrounding air and the speed and direction of any wind. The density is turn determined by the temperature, pressure, and humidity of the air. Lower temperatures, higher pressures, and lower humidity are all associated with higher density air. Denser air will produce greater lift, but will also produce more drag. Air pressure is most closely associated with altitude. In general, pressure decreases with altitude, so as you go higher up, the pressure of the surrounding air decreases.

With regard to wind, flying into the wind (headwind) has a similar type of impact to flying in denser air, though of much greater magnitude. In a headwind, the aircraft will have a higher speed relative to the surrounding air, which means it will experience greater drag and lift forces. Similarly, if the aircraft is flying the same direction as the wind (tailwind), it will have a lower speed relative to the surrounding air, and will experience reduced drag and lift.

Flight Concepts and Terminology

FLIGHT ATTITUDE

The flight attitude is described in terms of three axes, all of which meet at the plane's center of mass.

The **longitudinal** axis is the axis that extends from the center forward toward the nose and rearward toward the tail. The **lateral** axis extends from the center out to the right and left, perpendicular to the longitudinal axis. Typically the lateral axis passes through (over/under) the wings. Both of these axes are in the horizontal plane when the aircraft is level. The **vertical** axis meanwhile extends straight upward and downward from the aircraft's center, perpendicular to the other two axes. The motion of the aircraft can be described in relation to these axes: Rotation about the longitudinal axis is called roll; rotation about the lateral axis is called pitch; rotation about the vertical axis is called yaw. In turn, these three types of motion are controlled by three sets of flight control surfaces. Roll is controlled by the ailerons, pitch by the elevators, and yaw by the rudder. This information is summarized in the table below, and is expanded upon in the following section.

Axis	Motion	Control surface
Longitudinal	Roll	Ailerons
Lateral	Pitch	Elevators
Vertical	Yaw	Rudder

FLIGHT CONTROLS

Flight controls are divided into primary and secondary groups.

PRIMARY

The primary **flight control surfaces** are the ailerons, rudder, and elevator.

The **ailerons** are responsible for the roll, or movement around the longitudinal axis. The ailerons extend from the trailing edges of the wings as shown in the figure below and can be manipulated by the pilot to cause the wing to either dip below or elevate above the horizontal plane.

The joystick (or control wheel) controls the roll of the aircraft. By pushing the stick (or turning the wheel) to the left, the pilot raises the left aileron and lowers the right aileron, causing the left wing to dip and the right wing to elevate.

The **elevators** control the plane's pitch, or movement around the lateral axis. They are attached to the trailing edges of the horizontal stabilizers at the rear of the aircraft. Depending on the design of the plane, there may be one elevator that extends across the length of the horizontal stabilizer, or there may be two elevators, divided by the vertical stabilizer, as shown in the figure below. When the elevators are undivided, they are sometimes referred to as a stabilator.

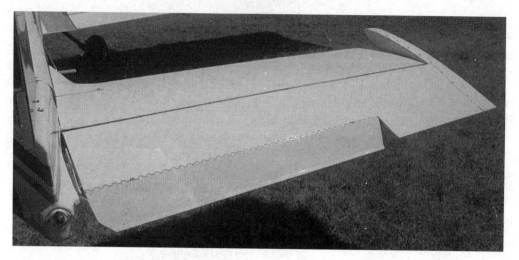

The joystick also controls the pitch of the aircraft. By pulling the stick back, the pilot raises the elevators, causing the tail of the plane to experience downward force, thus raising the nose of the plane. Pushing the stick forward will have the opposite effect on the elevators and will result in the nose of the plane dropping as the tail is pushed upward.

The **rudder** is a large flap attached by a hinge to the vertical stabilizer. It controls the motion of the plane around its vertical axis. The rudder can swing to the right or the left, causing the plane to turn (yaw) in either direction.

The rudder is controlled with two pedals: when the pilot pushes on the right pedal, the rudder swings out to the right, causing leftward pressure on the tail of the aircraft. This results in the nose of the plane turning to the right. Similarly, if the pilot pushes on the left pedal, the rudder will swing to the left, causing the tail to move right, and the nose to turn left.

The pilot also controls the amount of power or thrust being produced by the engines by manipulating the **throttle**. It is considered a primary flight control because the pilot must manage the thrust to ensure that the plane will be able to accomplish its intended maneuvers. With all three of the primary control surfaces, it is important to remember that the speed of the aircraft relative to the surrounding air determines the magnitude of the aircraft's response to the control. A plane that is traveling at 300 mph will roll much more quickly than one that is traveling at 200 mph in response to the same amount of aileron manipulation. The same is true of the other two types of motion.

Flight maneuvers usually involve the use of multiple controls. To make a proper turn, for instance, the pilot will need to employ the rudder, ailerons, and elevators. The bank is established by raising and lowering the ailerons, and the rudder pedals counteract any adverse yaw that occurs. Adverse yaw is the drifting of the nose caused by the extra drag on the downward-pointing aileron. Also, because extra lift is needed during a turn, the pilot must increase the angle of attack by applying downward elevator pressure. The amount of back elevator pressure required will be in proportion to the sharpness of the turn. This will be discussed in greater detail in the section on flight maneuvers.

SECONDARY

The secondary flight control surfaces include the flaps and leading edge devices, spoilers, and trim systems.

The **flaps** are connected to the trailing edges of the wings; they are raised or lowered to adjust the lift or drag. The retractable flaps on modern airplanes make it possible to cruise at a high speed and land at a low speed. On the opposite end of the wing, leading-edge devices accomplish much the same purpose. There are a number of different **leading-edge devices**: fixed slats, moveable slats, and leading edge flaps.

Spoilers are attached to the wings of some airplanes in order to diminish the lift and increase the drag. Spoilers can also be useful for roll control, in part because they reduce adverse yaw. This is accomplished by raising the spoiler on the side of the turn. This reduces the lift and creates more drag on that side, which causes that wing to drop and the plane to bank and yaw to that side. If both of the spoilers are raised at the same time, the plane can descend without increasing its speed. Raising the spoilers also improves the performance of the brakes, because they eliminate lift and push the plane down onto its wheels.

Trim systems exist mainly to ease the work of the pilot. They are attached to the trailing edges of one or more of the primary control surfaces. Small aircraft often have a single trim tab attached to the elevator. This tab is adjusted with a small wheel or crank, and its position is displayed in the cockpit. When the tab is deflected upwards, the trailing edge of the elevator is forced downward and the tail is pushed up, which lowers the nose of the plane.

Typically, a pilot first will achieve the desired pitch, power, attitude, and configuration, and then use the trim tabs to resolve the remaining control pressures. There are control pressures generated by any change in the flight condition, so trimming is necessary after any change. Trimming is complete when the pilot has eliminated any heaviness in the nose or tail of the plane.

Flight Maneuvers

The four basic maneuvers in flight are straight-and-level flight, turning, climbing, and descending. As the name suggests, **straight-and-level flight** involves keeping the aircraft headed in a particular direction at a particular altitude. Maintaining straight-and-level flight requires frequent adjustment, much the same way as the driver of a car has to make frequent adjustments to maintain a straight path on a windy day or when driving on a rough uneven road.

Making a smooth **turn** requires the use of all four primary controls: the throttle is set to achieve a speed suitable to the desired type of turn, the ailerons bank the wings and the elevators raise the nose to establish the rate of turn, and the rudder is employed to counter any undesired yaw resulting from the effects of the other controls or to introduce desired yaw.

There are three classes of turn: shallow, medium, and deep. A shallow turn has a bank of less than 20 degrees. At angles this shallow, most planes will tend to try to stabilize themselves back to a level angle, so the pilot must maintain some pressure on the stick to ensure that the plane doesn't pull out of the bank prematurely. A medium turn has a bank of roughly 20 to 45 degrees. Most planes will tend to stay in a medium bank until the pilot makes an adjustment. Finally, a steep turn is one in which the bank is greater than 45 degrees. For angles this steep, most planes will tend to try to increase the banking angle even further unless the pilot counters that tendency by maintaining some pressure on the stick in a stabilizing direction.

While the pilot is getting the plane to the desired bank angle, he will also be pulling back on the stick to ensure that the nose of the plane does not dip during the bank. This also serves to increase the rate at which the plane turns its heading. In general, the steeper the bank, the more sharply the pilot must pull back on the stick to maintain altitude. Because the lowered aileron on the raised wing generally creates more drag than the raised aileron on the lowered wing, the airplane tends to yaw in the direction opposite to the turn. For this reason, the pilot must at the same time apply rudder pressure in the direction of the turn.

To initiate a **climb**, an aircraft's nose is angled upward so that it gains altitude. Several things that remain constant while the aircraft is flying level change when the nose of the plane is raised. The two most significant are the effective angle of gravity and the angle of attack of the wings.

When the aircraft is level, **gravity** acts entirely in direction of the vertical axis of the plane. When the plane angles upward, the force of gravity, which still acts straight down like before, now has a component in the longitudinal direction, since the rear of the plane is now pointed slightly toward the ground. Additionally, since raising the noise of the aircraft increases the angle of attack of the wings, the amount of **drag** the aircraft experiences goes up considerably during a climb. This means that, in order to maintain flight, the thrust must now overcome both an increased amount of drag and part of the force of gravity.

If the nose of the aircraft is raised to quickly or without a sufficient increase in thrust to account for the changing flight conditions, the aircraft may **stall**. The most common cause of a stall is the plane not generating enough thrust to maintain air speed, which means that the lift being generated by the wings is not sufficient to keep the plane in the air, so the plane ceases to fly in a practical sense and instead begins to fall. To correct a stall, the pilot must angle the nose of the aircraft steeply downward and increase the throttle to generate enough airspeed in the forward direction so that the control surfaces are effective in controlling the flight of the plane again, and pull out of the dive. As should be apparent from this description, recovering from a stall involves significant loss of altitude, which makes stalling at low altitudes extremely dangerous.

There are a few different styles of controlled **descent**, but they all involve manipulation of the same two factors: **pitch** and **thrust**. By angling the nose of the plane downward, the pilot reduces the angle of attack of the wings and consequently reduces the amount of lift generated by the wings. This causes the plane to lose altitude. Similarly, by pulling back on the throttle, the pilot reduces the amount of thrust being generated, which in turn reduces the plane's air speed and the amount of lift generated by the wings, also resulting in a loss of altitude.

A **glide** is a controlled descent in which little or no engine power is used, and the plane drifts downward at a regular pace. The pilot manages a glide by balancing the forces of lift and gravity as they act on the plane.

When a pilot is executing a **landing**, the nose of the plane will actually be angled upward, but the throttle will be pulled way back to ensure that the plane continues its descent all the way to the ground.

Helicopters

In many ways, the operation of a helicopter is based on the same fundamentals as airplane flight. A helicopter is subject to the same four fundamental forces of lift, weight, thrust, and drag. Unlike an airplane, however, a helicopter applies most of its thrust vertically. When a helicopter flies at a constant speed in a stable horizontal path, the lift is equal to the weight and the forward thrust is equal to the drag. The helicopter will increase its horizontal speed if the thrust is greater than the drag, and will increase its altitude if the lift is greater than the weight. If the helicopter is hovering (i.e., not moving at all), there is no drag or forward thrust; only gravity and vertical thrust or lift, which are balanced.

The manner in which a helicopter generates lift is considerably different from that of an airplane. Whereas a plane derives its lift from the natural flow of air over the wing, the helicopter spins its "wing" rapidly and at a variable angle, giving it a variety of options for angles of attack. Because the main rotor of the helicopter is being torqued with such great force, it exerts the same amount of torque back on the fuselage of the helicopter but in the opposite direction (Newton's third law again). This necessitates a tail rotor to provide the force required to the keep the fuselage from spinning around while in flight. This function of the tail rotor is called **torque control**. Manipulation of the tail rotor is also used to change the heading of the helicopter.

HELICOPTER CONTROLS

Piloting a helicopter requires the use of three controls: the cyclic (stick), the collective, and the directional control system. The cyclic controls the longitudinal and lateral movement of the helicopter by adjusting the tilt of the main rotor. Moving the stick forward tilts the rotor forward, which in turn pushes the helicopter forward.

The collective is a tube running up from the cockpit floor to the left of the pilot. It has a handle that may be raised or lowered to affect the pitch, as well as a throttle that wraps around the handle and can be used to alter the engine torque. The collective controls the angle of the main rotor blades. If the handle is pulled up, the leading edge of the rotor blade lifts relative to the trailing edge.

The directional control system is a pair of pedals the pilot uses to alter the pitch of the tail rotor blades. Pressing one or the other of the pedals will cause the tail rotor to exert more or less force on the fuselage, which will in turn affect the heading of the helicopter.

A helicopter pilot must use all three of the controls at the same time. The cyclic and collective adjust the action of the main rotor, which must be compensated for with adjustment to the tail rotor. For instance, if the speed of the main rotor increases during a climb, the pilot will need to increase the amount of force generated by the tail rotor to ensure the fuselage does not begin to rotate.

If the helicopter loses engine power for some reason, the pilot will need to rely on autorotation, or the spinning of the rotors that is generated by airflow rather than the engine. The amount of torque on the fuselage will be smaller during autorotation, but it will still be enough to require the use of the tail rotor.

UNIQUE FORCES

A helicopter generates some other forces that distinguish it from an airplane. **Translational lift** is extra lift a helicopter experiences when traveling in a forward direction.

The **Coriolis force** is another physical phenomenon related to helicopters. The Coriolis force is the increase in rotational speed that occurs when the weight of a spinning object moves closer to the rotation center. In the case of a helicopter, having a greater portion of the weight closer to the base of the blade will cause the rotor to move faster, or to require less power to move at the same rotational speed.

If the main rotor increases the flow of air over the rear part of the main rotor disc, than the rear part will have a smaller angle of attack. The result of this will be less lift in the rear part of the rotor disc. This is called the **transverse flow effect**. However, when a force is applied to a spinning disc, the effects will occur ninety degrees later. This phenomenon is known as gyroscopic precession.

Airport Information

At an **airport**, the areas controlled by the aircraft traffic controller are called the movement (or maneuvering) areas. These include the runways and taxiways. Runways may be composed of all different materials, ranging from grass and dirt to asphalt and concrete. At a general aviation airport, the runways may be as little as 800 feet long and 26 feet wide, while an international airport may have runways that are 18,000 feet long and 260 feet across. The markings on a runway are white, but are usually outlined in black so that they may be better seen. Taxiways and areas not meant to be traveled by aircraft are marked in yellow.

There are three basic types of runway: visual, nonprecision instrument, and precision instrument. **Visual runways** are typical of small airports: they have no markings, though the boundaries and center lines may be indicated in some way. They are called visual runways because the pilot must be able to see the ground in order to land. It is not possible to land a plane on a visual runway simply with the use of instruments.

With a **nonprecision instrument runway**, a pilot may be able to make his approach using instruments. Specifically, this sort of runway can provide feedback on the horizontal position of the plane as it nears. Nonprecision instrument runways are commonly found at small and medium airports. These runways may have threshold markings, centerlines, and designators. These runways may also have a special mark, called an aiming point, between 1000 and 1500 feet long along the centerline of the runway.

Medium and large airports will have **precision instrument runways**, which give the pilot feedback on both horizontal and vertical position when the plane is on instrument approach. A precision instrument runway includes thresholds, designators, centerlines, aiming points, blast pads, stopways, and touchdown zone marks every 500 feet from the 500 foot to the 3000 foot mark.

Runways are named according to their **direction** on the compass, ranging from 01 to 36. So, for instance, due south would be runway 18 ("one-eight"), and due west would be runway 27 ("two-seven"). In North America, the runways are named in accordance with geographic (grid) north, rather than magnetic north. Of course, a runway may have two names, one for each direction in which it is used. The same runway may be referred to as runway 05 ("zero-five") or runway 23 ("two-three") depending on the direction it is being used on a given day. In most cases, fixed-wing aircraft take off and land against the wind, because the extra amount of air over the wing will increase lift (and reduce the required ground speed).

In the event that **multiple runways** travel in the same direction, they will be distinguished from each other by their relative positions according to an observer on approach from the appropriate direction: left or right runway if there are only two; left, right, or center runway if there are three. Of course, a runway that is on the right when travelling in one direction will be on the left when it is being used in the opposite direction.

In most cases, **runway lights** are operated by the airport control tower. There are a number of different components to a runway lighting system. A Runway Centerline Lighting System is a line of white lights mounted every fifty feet along the centerline. When the approaching plane gets within 3000 feet of the runway, the lights begin to blink red and white; when the plane gets within 1000 feet, the lights become solid red. Precision instrument runways have runway end lights and edge lights. Runway end lights run the width of both ends of the runway: from the ground these lights appear red, while they appear green from above. Runway edge lights run the length of the runway on both sides. This lighting typically changes color as well when the plane gets within a certain distance of the front end of the runway. There are similar lights marking the boundaries of taxiways. An Approach Lighting System is a set of strobelights and/or lightbars that indicate the end of the runway from which descending aircraft should arrive. Runway end identification lights are synchronized lights that flash at the runway thresholds. At some airports these lights face in every direction, while at others they only face the direction from which planes approach. Runway end identification lights are useful when the runway doesn't stand out from the surrounding area, or when visibility is poor.

Some big airports also have **Visual Approach Slope Indicators**, which give the incoming pilot useful information. In a typical VASI system, white lights indicate the lower glide path limits and red lights indicate the upper. The VASI should be visible for twenty miles at night, and for three to five miles during the day under normal conditions. An effective VASI should keep the plane clear of obstructions so long as it remains within approximately ten degrees of the extended runway centerline and within four nautical miles of the runway threshold.

Nautical Information

Naval air operations play a crucial role in America's national defense systems, and have done so since 1922 when the USS *Jupiter* was converted into the USS *Langley*, America's first aircraft carrier. Deployed in both combat and non-combat missions, they carry both rotary and fixed wing aircraft.

There are two main types of aircraft carriers in use: CATOBAR, which stands for Catapult Assisted Take-off But Arrested Recovery or Catapult Assisted Take-off Barrier Arrested Recovery, and STOVL, which stands for Short Take-Off and Vertical Landing. Of the 19 aircraft carriers currently in use in America, ten are CATOBAR, and nine are STOVL. They are listed below:

CATOBAR	STOVL
Nimitz (CVN*)	America (LHA**)
Dwight D. Eisenhower (CVN)	Wasp (LHD***)
Carl Vinson (CVN)	Essex (LHD)
Theodore Roosevelt (CVN)	Kearsarge (LHD)
Abraham Lincoln (CVN)	Boxer (LHD)
George Washington (CVN)	Bataan (LHD)
John C. Stennis (CVN)	Bonhomme Richard (LHD)
Harry S. Truman (CVN)	Iwo Jima (LHD)
Ronald Reagan (CVN)	Makin Island (LHD)
George H.W. Bush (CVN)	

*CVN's are nuclear powered aircraft carriers. The letters stand for Cruiser, Volare (which is Italian for "flight"), and Nuclear.

**LHA stands for Landing Helicopter Assault.

***LHD stands for Landing Helicopter Dock.

The head of the aircraft operations crew on a carrier is the Air Officer, who is often referred to as the air boss. He works out of the Primary Flight Control tower, also known as PriFly, along with his assistant, who is known as the miniboss. Both usually wear yellow, but as head of all operations, the Air Officer is free to wear any of the crew colors. Together they are responsible for all aircraft operations on a carrier, and for any craft in the air within a radius of five nautical miles.

Catapult officers man the powerful mechanisms that allow planes on aircraft carriers to go from 0 to 165 MPH in two seconds. Catapult officers are also known as shooters.

The Aircraft Handling Officer, or ACHO, works in Flight Deck Control. The ACHO's job is to keep the various aircraft on the carrier in such a way as to facilitate as much as possible quick takeoffs and landings, while striving at all times to prevent the occurrence of a "locked deck." This takes place when so many aircraft are out of order that no more can land until some of the ones on deck are rearranged.

The Landing Signal Officer (LSO) guides pilots as they bring the aircraft back in for landing, using both hand signals and radio. They are always experienced pilots, as they must instantly be able to judge whether there's any problems with an incoming craft's approach angle, lineup, or altitude.

The Arresting Gear Office (AGO) is in charge of operating the system of massive cables that brings the aircraft to a rapid halt. He or she also decides if the deck is *clear* or *foul* – clear being ready for a landing and foul being unready.

Uniforms on aircraft carriers signify both rank and job assignment. On flight decks, junior sailor and petty officers wear navy blue pants; warrant officer, commissioned officers, and chief petty officers wear khaki pants. In addition, members of flight crews on aircraft carriers wear deck jerseys, float coats, and helmets in different colors that signify their jobs.

Here are the color codes:

- *Purple*
  - Aviation Fuels
- *Blue*
  - Plane Handlers
  - Aircraft elevator Operators
  - Tractor Drivers
  - Messengers and Phone Talkers
- *Green*
  - Catapult and arresting gear crews
  - Air wing maintenance personnel
  - Cargo-handling personnel
  - Ground Support Equipment (GSE) troubleshooters
  - Hook runners
  - Photographer's Mates
  - Helicopter landing signal enlisted personnel (LSE)
- *Yellow*
  - Aircraft handling officers

- Catapult and Arresting Gear Officers
- Plane directors
- *Red*
  - Ordnancemen
  - Crash and Salvage Crews
  - Explosive Ordnance Disposal (EOD)
- *Brown*
  - Air wing plane captains
  - Air wing line leading petty officers
- *White*
  - Quality Assurance (QA)
  - Squadron plane inspectors
  - Landing signal officer (LSO)
  - Air transfer officers (ATO)
  - Liquid oxygen (LOX) crews
  - Safety observers
  - Medical personnel
- *White/black*
  - Final checker (inspector)

Takeoffs and landings on aircraft carriers generally occur in cycles of several aircraft at a time. This is known as the launch and recovery cycle. These cycles generally last around 90 minutes, and typically involve 15-20 aircraft, and each cycle is known as an *event*. An event starts with one group of aircraft being arranged so that each aircraft can take off in sequence with no delay needed to move them into the correct position. This is known as *spotting*. They are then launched, and about an hour later, another group of aircraft will go through the same process. Shortly after the second group finishes launching, the first group will begin landing. Not long after that, the second group will begin landing, and a new event will start.

There are three types, or *cases*, of takeoffs and landings. Which one is used depends on weather and environment:

- Case I is used when instrument conditions are not expected, it is daylight, the ceiling around the carrier is at least 3,000 feet, and visibility is at least five nautical miles.
- Case II is used when instrument conditions may occur during the flight, the ceiling around the carrier is at least 1,000 feet, and visibility is at least five nautical miles.
- Case III is used during night operations, or when it is very likely that instrument conditions will occur because the ceiling is lower than 1,000 feet, or visibility is less than five nautical miles.

Naval Acronyms

Acronym	Meaning
AO	Aviation Ordnanceman
APG	Advanced Pay Grade -Opportunity to advance to a higher pay grade based on previously obtained experience.
ASTB	Aviation Selection Test Battery
ASVAB	Armed Services Vocational Aptitude Battery -Test administered by the military to determine qualification for enlistment in the Armed Forces.

Acronym	Meaning
BMT	Basic Military Training - Initial instruction given to new military personnel.
BS	Battle Stations - The final test at Boot Camp that determines the passage to becoming a U.S. Navy Sailor. On board ship, a location and conditions to respond to when under attack or experiencing an emergency such as a fire.
BUD/S	Basic Underwater Demolition/SEAL - A SEAL training course that develops mental and physical stamina as well as leadership skills.
BUPERS	Bureau of Navy Personnel - Organization served to provide administrative leadership, policy planning and general oversight of the Navy.
CB	Construction Battalion (Seabees) - The Navy community of construction workers.
CDR	Commander - Navy Senior Officer rank (0–5).
CEC	Civil Engineer Corps - Officer corps that oversees the construction, renovation, maintenance and building of Navy projects all over the world.
CNO	Chief of Naval Operations - The highest ranking Officer in the U.S. Navy.
CO	Commanding Officer - A commissioned Navy Officer in charge of a designated Navy command.
CREO	Career Reenlistment Objectives
CTI	Cryptologic Technicians Interpretive - Navy linguists tasked to gather highly classified intelligence information for the Navy's top-level decision makers using foreign language skills.
DD214	DD Form 214 - Certificate of release or discharge from Active Duty.
DEP	Delayed Entry Program - Program that allows recruits to join the Navy but postpone reporting for duty for up to a year.
DLA	Dislocation Allowance - Money provided to Sailors to aid in moves from one duty station to another.
DMI	Departmental Material Inspection - An inspection of bed making, folding and stowing of gear.
DOD	Department of Defense - Federal department in charge of organizing and supervising all agencies related directly to national defense, specifically the Armed Forces.
DON	Department of the Navy - Department established by Congress to provide support and leadership to the U.S. Navy.
DT	Dental Technician - Enlisted Sailor tasked with assisting Navy Dentists in providing dental care to Navy personnel and their families.
EAOS	End of Active Obligated Service - Date at which one's Naval service has been officially completed.
ENL	Enlisted - Rank achieved by Sailors who have completed the minimum educational requirement of a high school diploma.
EOD	Explosive Ordnance Disposal - Technicians tasked to safely dispose of explosive materials.
FAC	Forward Air Controller - An individual who directs the action of military aircraft engaged in close air support of land forces.
FMF	Fleet Marine Force
HM	Hospital Corpsman - Enlisted Sailor tasked with assisting Navy Medical Officers in providing medical care to Navy and Marine Corps personnel and their families.
IT	Information Technology - Naval community made up of communications experts who process, transmit and analyze a wide variety of data.
JAG	Judge Advocate General - Corps that provides legal services and advice in all legal matters involving the Navy or the Command.
JTF	Joint Task Force - The combination of more than one military service.

Acronym	Meaning
LSO	Landing Signal Officer - Naval Aviators specifically trained to facilitate the safe recovery of aircraft aboard aircraft carriers.
MAVNI	Military Accessions Vital to the National Interest
MCPON	Master Chief Petty Officer of the Navy - The senior most Enlisted member of the U.S. Navy.
MEPS	Military Entrance Processing Station - Station where recruits take the ASVAB, physical exam, select a rating and take the Oath of Enlistment.
MSC	Medical Service Corps - Navy Officer Corps consisting of health-care administrators, optometrists, pharmacists, scientists and other specialized practitioners.
NEX	The Navy Exchange - A department store for military personnel and their families.
NFO	Naval Flight Officer - Officer who specializes in aircraft weapons and sensor systems (2nd seat in the cockpit).
NKO	Navy Knowledge Online – www.nko.navy.mil
NROWS	Navy Reserve Order Writing System
NPS	Non-Prior Service - Someone without any previous military experience.
NRC	Navy Recruiting Command - Main headquarters for Navy recruiting, located in Millington, Tennessee.
NROTC	Naval Reserve Officers Training Corps - A college scholarship program used to recruit future commissioned Officers for the Navy and Marine Corps.
NSAWC	Naval Strike and Air Warfare Center - Provides training and service to aircrews and squadrons.
OCS	Officer Candidate School - A 12-week training program designed to give Officers a working knowledge of the Navy. It is the equivalent to Officer Boot Camp.
OIC	Officer in Charge - A commissioned Navy Officer in charge of an organization, facility or function, responsible for a group of Officers and Sailors in the organization.
PAO	Public Affairs Officer - Officer responsible for preparing and disseminating information relative to military operations through news releases, photographs, radio and television, and other informational material.
PFA	Physical Fitness Assessment - A required basic physical test conducted to determine the physical fitness of Navy personnel.
PI	Personal Inspections - An inspection of a recruit's personal appearance and uniform.
PIR	Pass-in-review - Boot Camp graduation.
PRD	Projected Rotation Date - Date on which a Navy Officer or Sailor's next duty station is established based on their pay grade and community.
PRT	Physical Readiness Test - A required basic physical test conducted to determine the physical fitness of Navy personnel.
RDC	Recruit Drill/Division Commander - Sailor responsible for training recruits at the Navy Recruit Training Command (RTC).
RL	Restricted Line - A Line Officer is a commissioned Officer who is not eligible for sea command.
RTC	Recruit Training Command - Campus located in Great Lakes, Illinois, where Navy recruits train to become Sailors. Also known as Boot Camp.
SEAL	Sea-Air-Land (Team) - Members of the Navy Special Operations Force who specialize in direct action and special reconnaissance missions.
SECNAV	Secretary of the Navy - Civilian head of the Department of the Navy, responsible for conducting all affairs related to the Department.
SIQ	Sick In Quarters - Term used when a medical condition or injury is such that in-hospital care is not required to return the patient to a full- or limited-duty status.

Acronym	Meaning
SWCC	Special Warfare Combatant-Craft Crewman (pronounced: swick) - Navy Special Operations Force member who operates the inventory of boats used for mission support.
SWO	Surface Warfare Officer - Navy Officer Corps who pilot, operate and manage a surface ship such as destroyers and cruisers.
TAD	Temporary Additional Duty - A temporary assignment of additional duty.
UCMJ	Uniform Code of Military Justice - The foundation of all military law in the United States, applicable to all members of uniformed services of the United States.
URL	Unrestricted Line Officer - Officer of the line in the U.S. Navy who is qualified to command ships, subs and aviation units and can rise to high Navy leadership positions such as CNO.
USN	United States Navy - The sea branch of the U.S. Armed Forces.
USNA	United States Naval Academy - The undergraduate college in Annapolis, Maryland, that educates and commissions Navy Officers and Marine Corps Officers.
WSO	Weapons System Officer - Specific to the F/A-18F and F/A-18D aircrafts, an Officer who specializes in airborne weapons and sensor systems.
XO	Executive Officer - Naval Officer who is second in command, reporting to the Commanding Officer (CO).

Naval Terms

Term	Meaning
ADRIFT	Loose from moorings and out of control. Applied to anything lost or out of hand.
AFT	Towards the stern (tail) of a ship.
ALL HANDS	The entire ship's company, both Officer and Enlisted.
ALLOTMENT	An amount of money a Sailor has coming out of regular pay.
AVIATION BOATSWAIN'S MATE	Aviation Boatswain's Mates (AB) work with naval aircraft on land and on flight decks at sea, specializing in anything from aircraft launch and recovery (ABE) to aircraft fueling (ABF) to aircraft handling (ABH).
AYE, AYE	Response acknowledging the understanding of a command/statement.
BARRACKS	A building where Sailors live when ashore.
BELOW	Downstairs, like the next deck below.
BLACKSHOE	Non-aviation rate for Enlisted personnel as well as Officers. A "shoe" is a ship driver/Surface Warfare Officer.
BLUE NOSE	A Sailor who has crossed either the Arctic or Antarctic Circle. Also applies to Officers.
BOATWAIN'S MATE	The oldest rate in the Navy, Boatswain's Mates (BM) are "jack-of-all-trades" Sailors who perform general seamanship duties on board Navy ships – everything from ship maintenance to loading/unloading cargo and supplies.
BOW	The forward part of a ship or boat.
BRIGHTWORK	Brass or shiny metal kept polished rather than painted.
BROWNSHOE	Aviation rate Enlisted personnel.
BULKHEAD	The wall.
BUNK	A bed.
BUOY	An anchored float used as an aid to navigation or to mark the location of an object.
CARRY ON	An order to resume work or duties.
CAST OFF	To throw off, to let go, to unfurl.
CHAIN LOCKER	Compartment in which anchor chain is stowed.

Term	Meaning
CHIT	Forms used to request taking leave, a day off, etc.
CHIT BOOK	Coupon or receipt booklet.
CHOW HALL	(MESS DECK) A place to eat.
COLORS	Raising and lowering of the National Ensign, the American flag and organization flags.
CUP OF JOE	A cup of coffee. Named after Josephus Daniels, Secretary of the Navy 1913–1921, who under General Order 99 in June 1914 prohibited the use of alcohol on board U.S. Navy ships.
DECK	The floor.
DEEP SIX	To dispose of or throw away.
ENLISTED	The general work force of the Navy and Navy Reserve – generally requires a high school diploma (or GED) as a minimum educational requirement, completion of Recruit Training and training in an occupational specialty area.
ENSIGN	The rank of an Officer between Chief Warrant Officer and Lieutenant Junior Grade.
FAST	Snugly secured.
FATHOM	A unit of length equal to 6 feet used for measuring the depth of water.
FIELD DAY	Full-blown cleaning, sort of like spring cleaning in overdrive.
FIRST LIEUTENANT	The Officer responsible to the XO for the deck department/division aboard ship.
FLAG OFFICER	Any commissioned Officer in pay grade 0–7 or above.
GALLEY	The kitchen.
GANGWAY	An opening in the bulwark or lifeline that provides access to a brow or accommodation ladder; when shouted means to get out of the way.
GEAR LOCKER	A storage room.
GEEDUNK	Candy, gum or cafeteria, sometimes called pogey bait.
GENERAL QUARTERS	Battle Stations.
GRAD AND GO	A Boot Camp graduate who leaves for the next duty station three hours after graduation.
GROUND TACKLE	The equipment used in mooring or anchoring a ship.
HATCH	The door.
HEAD	The restroom.
JACK BOX	Access box to sound-powered phone circuitry.
LADDER	A device to move personnel from one level to another. Stairs.
LEAVE	Authorized absence, like vacation.
LIBERTY	Permission to leave the base, usually for not more than 48 hours.
LIFELINE	Lines erected around the weather decks of a ship to prevent personnel from falling or being washed over the side.
MARLINSPIKE	A life-size model ship where recruits practice mooring, line handling, putting out to sea and other aspects of basic seamanship.
MESS DECK	The crew's dining area.
MESS DUTY	A 90-day obligated duty working on the mess decks when first reporting aboard. (aka MESS-CRANK'N)
MID-WATCH	The midnight watch, the most dreaded watch because one loses the most sleep out of the rotation.
NAVY RESERVE	Reserve component of the U.S. Navy in which part-time Sailors and Officers are called into Active Duty, or mobilized, as needed.

Term	Meaning
OFFICER	The leadership and management team of the Navy and Navy Reserve – generally requires a degree from a four-year college or university and completion of an Officer Training program.
OMBUDSMAN	Volunteer who is the well-trained link between Sailors and their families.
OVERHEAD	The ceiling.
P-DAYS	"Processing days." When recruits first arrive at Boot Camp, they are issued initial equipment, uniforms and supplies.
PASSAGEWAY	A hallway.
PORT	A place on a waterway with facilities for loading and unloading ships.
PORT SIDE	The left side of a nautical vessel.
QUARTERS	Assembling all hands for muster. Also refers to a home on base, a residence.
RACK	A bed.
RATING	A job specialty title.
REVEILLE	A signal signifying the start of a workday.
RICKY	A recruit.
SCULLERY	A place to wash dishes.
SCUTTLEBUTT	Originally meant to describe a water fountain. Quickly became a place Sailors would gather and talk. Term now used primarily for rumors and rumor control.
SECURE	To stop or quit work.
SICK BAY	Medical facility located in a hospital, aid station or on board ship.
SNIPE	Anyone who works in the Engineering department.
STARBOARD	The right side of a nautical vessel.
STERN	The aft part (rear) of a ship or boat.
SWEEPERS	Cleaning ritual that involves sweeping assigned areas.
SWAB	A mop.
TAPS	Lights out, time for sleep.
TURN TO	Begin work.
WORKING ALOFT	Working above the highest deck, generally performing maintenance on the ship's mast.

The Other Subtests

Naval Aviation Trait Facet Inventory (NATFI)

The Naval Aviation Trait Facet Inventory (NATFI) subtest is not something a person can study for. It's a personality profile, and a specific type of personality profile at that – it's an ipsative, or "forced choice" test. This simply means that for each of the 88 questions in this section, you'll be given two choices, and asked which one you prefer. In many cases, the two choices will seem to be completely unrelated. For example:

With which of these statements do you most strongly agree?
   a. I am most productive in the morning
   b. I enjoy watching sports

Even if you never watch sports, and are far more productive in the afternoon than in the morning, you will have to choose one of the two alternatives, as you can't leave an answer blank. You will encounter many questions where neither alternative is really satisfactory, but you will always have to pick one.

Be aware that you should never select an answer because it's the one you think the military is looking for. Standardized personality testing is extremely sophisticated, and the developers of the NATFI have devised nearly foolproof ways of determining if a person is being honest throughout the test, or is just trying to give the "right" answer on some questions.

This subtest is used to determine which candidates possess the specific personality traits necessary for a successful career in military aviation. Therefore, a test taker who is seen as blatantly attempting to game the test by telling the military what he or she thinks they want to hear will most likely not be viewed as a suitable candidate, no matter how well they do on the other sections of the ASTB. You should do your best to be as honest as possible when answering the questions in this section, no matter how frustrating they may be.

Performance Based Measures (PBM)

The Performance Based Measures (PBM) subsection of the ASTB-E is a hands-on test of reaction time, dexterity, focus, and multitasking ability. It is actually much like a video game, so it's not something you can really study for, at least not in the traditional sense. There are several sections on this subtest, and some of them overlap. While taking the PBM, you'll be using headphones, a joystick, and a throttle. Skills being tested include dichotic listening, digit cancellation, multi-tracking, vertical tracking, airplane tracking, and responding in emergency scenarios

The first section sounds simple enough, but is harder than it first appears. You'll be shown a map, with North at the top, and you'll be shown in which direction your airborne craft is heading. From this perspective, you'll be looking down at a building, with a parking lot on each of the north, south, east, and west sides of the building. These parking lots won't be labeled by direction, and you'll be asked to identify in which direction from the building one of the lots is. You'll do this repeatedly, but each time your aircraft's direction and the designated parking lot will change. Questions come very quickly, meaning you won't have much time to think about your response.

You may find the second section to be somewhat familiar. At some point in your life, possibly at school, you have probably taken a hearing test in which you don headphones and then signal to the examiner in which ear you're hearing a sound. On this test, you'll be told to listen for a number to be spoken in one ear. If that number is odd, you'll click a button on the throttle, but if it's even, you'll press a button on the joystick. That sounds easy enough, but then it starts to get complicated, as you'll start hearing numbers and letters, and they'll be in both ears, but you'll still be required to respond only to numbers, and only in the correct ear, and to make the appropriate response for odd or even numbers.

In the next section, just as with the previous one, you'll start with a fairly simple task, but it becomes more difficult as you progress. At first, you'll see a small airplane moving up and down in a straight line on the far left side of the monitor. Your job is to use your throttle to keep your gunsight directly over the aircraft at all times. After that, the aircraft will begin moving over the entire screen, and you'll need to use your joystick to keep your gunsight over it. Then, you'll need to use either your joystick or your throttle as the aircraft's movement become even more complicated and faster. Next, you'll be listening to letters and numbers being spoken in your ears from the previous test, and you'll need to be able to multitask very well to handle this challenge. That's not the end of it; you'll be given instructions on what to do in case of an emergency, and then you'll be tested on your accuracy and speed at responding correctly when you're informed of emergencies later. Needless to say, PBM is a very difficult test to do well in, so don't get too discouraged if you feel like you had a less than stellar performance. The military is trying to determine your aptitude, or potential for learning, in these areas, not whether or not you are already highly skilled in them.

Biographical Inventory with Response Verification (BI-RV)

The Biographical Inventory with Response Verification (BI-RV) is not a test in the traditional sense of the word. You won't take it in the APEX testing environment, and you don't need to be supervised while taking it. The title of the subtest is pretty self-explanatory – you'll list important experiences and achievements from your life history. They don't have to be directly relevant to a career as a military aviator. Items to include would include your high school GPA, any scholastic honors or awards, extracurricular activities, volunteer efforts, etc. It's best to have this part of the ASTB completed before you sit down to take the rest of the test.

You'll also expected to give details that can be used to verify your experiences, such as the years you attended a school, the name of your football coach, the volunteer coordinator at the soup kitchen you served at, etc. That's where the "response verification" part comes into play. The military probably won't attempt to verify the truth and accuracy of every entry on your BI-RV, but they have the right to, and will probably verify at least some of the items. If any of them turn out to be false, or exaggerated, you can be rejected by the military. This isn't just during the application process, either – if it's *ever* discovered that you lied or exaggerated on the BI-RV you can be discharged immediately, even if it's not found out until you've been in the military for years. So it's very important to be completely honest and as precise as possible.

Final Notes

This concludes our review of the content of the ASTB-E subtests. Hopefully, a lot of this material was familiar to you, but if not, be sure to reread any sections you had difficulty with until you have a solid grasp of the important concepts. As you read, try to imagine the types of questions that will be asked on the test, and take frequent breaks to let the ideas sink in.

The ASTB-E tests a wide variety of knowledge and skills, so getting prepared for it is necessarily a difficult task, but so is training to be a pilot. If you can work hard enough to ace the ASTB-E, that's enough to convince the military you're a good bet to make it through flight training.

Good luck and good studying!

ASTB-E Practice Test

Math Skills Test

1. If 16x + 4 = 100, what is the value of x?

   a. 6
   b. 7
   c. 8
   d. 9

2. Simplify the following expression:

     $(2x - 20)(5x + 10)$

   a. $10x^2 - 80x - 200$
   b. $70x - 200$
   c. $10x^2 - 80x + 200$
   d. $10x^2 - 120x - 200$

3. Which of the following are complementary angles?

   a. 71° and 19°
   b. 90° and 90°
   c. 90° and 45°
   d. 15° and 30°

4. Simply the following expression:

     $(2x^4)^3 + 2(y^5)^5$

   a. $8x^{64} + 2y^{3125}$
   b. $6x^7 + 2y^{10}$
   c. $6x^{12} + 2y^{25}$
   d. $8x^{12} + 2y^{25}$

5. If the measures of the three angles in a triangle are 2 : 6 : 10, what is the measure of the smallest angle?

   a. 20 degrees
   b. 40 degrees
   c. 60 degrees
   d. 80 degrees

6. If a circle has a diameter of 12cm, what is its area?

   a. 38cm²
   b. 113cm²
   c. 276cm²
   d. 452cm²

7. The length of a square is 15cm. What is its area?

   a. 30cm²
   b. 60cm²
   c. 150cm²
   d. 225cm²

8. A rectangular solid measures 12cm by 3cm by 9cm. What is its volume?

   a. $36cm^3$
   b. $108cm^3$
   c. $324cm^3$
   d. $407cm^3$

9. If $2x^2 = -4x^2 + 216$, what is the value of x?

   a. 4
   b. 5
   c. 6
   d. 7

10. The perimeter of a square is 24 m. What is its area?

   a. $30m^2$
   b. $36m^2$
   c. $42m^2$
   d. $24m^2$

11. If a rectangle has a length of 5cm and a width of 7cm, what is its area?

   a. $24cm^2$
   b. $35cm^2$
   c. $42cm^2$
   d. $56cm^2$

12. On a six-sided die, each side has a number between 1 and 6. What is the probability of throwing a 3 or a 4?

   a. 1 in 6
   b. 1 in 3
   c. 1 in 2
   d. 1 in 4

13. Solve for y in the following inequality:

     $-2y \geq 24 + 6$

   a. $y \leq 15$
   b. $y \geq 15$
   c. $y \leq -15$
   d. $y \geq -15$

14. If $2x = 5x - 30$, what is the value of x?

   a. 10
   b. -10
   c. 4.3
   d. -4.3

15. Given the functions, $f(x) = 3x + 6$ and $g(x) = 2x - 8$, what is the solution of the equation, $f(x) = g(x)$?

 a. $x = -12$
 b. $x = -8$
 c. $x = -14$
 d. $x = -10$

16. Suppose the area of the square in the diagram to the right is 64 in². (The square is not shown actual size.) What is the area of the circle?

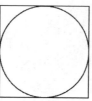

 a. 16π in^2
 b. 64π in^2
 c. $\frac{64}{\pi}$ in^2
 d. $(64 + \pi)$ in^2

17. Solve for x in the following inequality:

 4x + 23 > -3x – 6

 a. x > -4.14
 b. x < -4.14
 c. x > 4.14
 d. x < 4.14

18. If 2x + 5x = 3x + x + 30, what is the value of x?

 a. 2.72
 b. 4.29
 c. 6
 d. 10

19. 3x²y + y/2 – 6x

 If x=4 and y=10, what is the value of the expression

 a. 221
 b. 461
 c. 872
 d. 1916

20. At a school carnival, three students spend an average of $10. Six other students spend an average of $4. What is the average amount of money spent by all nine students?

 a. $5
 b. $6
 c. $7
 d. $8

21. If w=7, calculate the value of the following expression:

$$8w^2 - 12w + (4w - 5) + 6$$

   a. 279
   b. 285
   c. 337
   d. 505

22. If x/3 + 7 = 35, what is the value of x?

   a. 9.33
   b. 14
   c. 84
   d. 126

23. In the following equation, solve for x by factoring:

$$2x^2 - 7x = x^2 - 12$$

   a. x = -3, -4
   b. x = 3, 4
   c. x = 3, -4
   d. x = -3, 4

24. If x is 25% of 250, what is the value of x?

   a. 62.5
   b. 100
   c. 1000
   d. 6250

25. Which of the following inequalities is correct?

   a. $\frac{1}{3} < \frac{2}{7} < \frac{5}{12}$
   b. $\frac{2}{7} < \frac{1}{3} < \frac{5}{12}$
   c. $\frac{5}{12} < \frac{2}{7} < \frac{1}{3}$
   d. $\frac{5}{12} < \frac{1}{3} < \frac{2}{7}$

26. If the volume of a cube is 8cm³, what is the length of the cube?

   a. 1cm
   b. 2cm
   c. 3cm
   d. 4cm

27. Simply the following expression:

$$(2x^2 + 3)(2x - 1)$$

   a. $4x^3 - 2x^2 + 6x - 3$
   b. $2x^2 + 6x - 3$
   c. $4x^3 - 2x^2 + 6x + 3$
   d. $4x^3 - 2x^2 - 6x - 3$

28. Simply the following expression

$$(2x^4y^7m^2z) * (5x^2y^3m^8)$$

   a. $10x^6y^9m^{10}z$
   b. $7x^6y^{10}m^{10}z$
   c. $10x^5y^{10}m^{10}z$
   d. $10x^6y^{10}m^{10}z$

29. A classroom contains 13 boys and 18 girls. If a student's name is chosen randomly, what is the probability it will be a girl's name?

   a.   36%
   b.   42%
   c.   58 %
   d.   72%

30. What is 10% of 40%?

   a.   4%
   b.   30%
   c.   50%
   c.   400%

Reading Comprehension Test

Use the passage below to answer the following two questions:

Inside the cockpit, three key items to be checked are: (1) battery and ignition switches—off, (2) control column locks—removed, (3) landing gear control— down and locked.

The fuel selectors should be checked for proper operation in all positions—including the OFF position. Stiff selectors, or ones where the tank position is hard to find, are unacceptable. The primer should also be exercised. The pilot should feel resistance when the primer is both pulled out and pushed in. The primer should also lock securely. Faulty primers can interfere with proper engine operation. The engine controls should also be manipulated by slowly moving each through its full range to check for binding or stiffness.

The airspeed indicator should be properly marked, and the indicator needle should read zero. If it does not, the instrument may not be calibrated correctly. Similarly, the vertical speed indicator (VSI) should also read zero when the airplane is on the ground. If it does not, a small screwdriver can be used to zero the instrument. The VSI is the only flight instrument that a pilot has the prerogative to adjust. All others must be adjusted by an FAA certificated repairman or mechanic.

1. According to the passage, which of the following setting configurations is correct?

a.
Battery and ignition switches: On
Control column locks: Removed
Landing gear control: Down and locked
Airspeed Indicator needle: 0
b.
Battery and ignition switches: Off
Control column locks: Removed
Landing gear control: Up and locked
Airspeed Indicator needle: 0
c.
Battery and ignition switches: On
Control column locks: In place
Landing gear control: Up and locked
Airspeed Indicator needle: 0
d.
Battery and ignition switches: Off
Control column locks: Removed
Landing gear control: Down and locked
Airspeed Indicator needle: 0

2. In the passage, what does the word *primer* mean?

a. Short, introductory guide
b. Small fuel pump
c. Painted binding agent
d. Explosive ignition cap

Use the passage below to answer the following question:

Radial engines were widely used during World War II and many are still in service today. With these engines, a row or rows of cylinders are arranged in a circular pattern around the crankcase. The main advantage of a radial engine is the favorable power-to-weight ratio. In-line engines have a comparatively small frontal area, but their power-to-weight ratios are relatively low. In addition, the rearmost cylinders of an air-cooled, in-line engine receive very little cooling air, so these engines are normally limited to four or six cylinders. V-type engines provide more horsepower than in-line engines and still retain a small frontal area.

3. According to this passage, how much use did in-line engines get during World War II?
   a. None at all
   b. A limited amount of use
   c. Quite a bit of use
   d. The article doesn't say

Use the passage below to answer the following question:

It takes only one harrowing experience to clarify the distinction between minimum practical knowledge and a thorough understanding of how to apply the procedures and techniques used in instrument flight. Your instrument training is never complete; it is adequate when you have absorbed every foreseeable detail of knowledge and skill to ensure a solution will be available if and when you need it.

4. In this passage, harrowing means:
   a. Rapidly descending
   b. Extremely disturbing
   c. Extremely unprepared
   d. Last minute

Use the passage below to answer the following two questions:

One disadvantage of the float-type carburetor is its icing tendency. Carburetor ice occurs due to the effect of fuel vaporization and the decrease in air pressure in the venturi, which causes a sharp temperature drop in the carburetor. If water vapor in the air condenses when the carburetor temperature is at or below freezing, ice may form on internal surfaces of the carburetor, including the throttle valve. The reduced air pressure, as well as the vaporization of fuel, contributes to the temperature decrease in the carburetor. Ice generally forms in the vicinity of the throttle valve and in the venturi throat. This restricts the flow of the fuel/air mixture and reduces power. If enough ice builds up, the engine may cease to operate. Carburetor ice is most likely to occur when temperatures are below 70 degrees Fahrenheit (°F) or 21 degrees Celsius (°C) and the relative humidity is above 80 percent. Due to the sudden cooling that takes place in the carburetor, icing can occur even with temperatures as high as 100 °F (38 °C) and humidity as low as 50 percent. This temperature drop can be as much as 60 to 70 °F (15 to 21 °C). Therefore, at an outside air temperature of 100 °F (37 °C), a temperature drop of 70 °F (21 °C) results in an air temperature in the carburetor of 30 °F (-1 °C).

5. Which set of conditions would allow carburetor icing to occur?
   a. 50 degrees Fahrenheit and 50% relative humidity
   b. 90 degrees Fahrenheit and 40% relative humidity
   c. 75 degrees Fahrenheit and 60% relative humidity
   d. 80 degrees Fahrenheit and 30% relative humidity

6. In which set of conditions would carburetor icing be most likely to occur?
   a. 50 degrees Fahrenheit and 75% relative humidity
   b. 60 degrees Fahrenheit and 85% relative humidity
   c. 75 degrees Fahrenheit and 60% relative humidity
   d. 850 degrees Fahrenheit and 30% relative humidity

Use the passage below to answer the following question:

It is impossible to emphasize too strongly the necessity for forming correct habits in flying straight and level. All other flight maneuvers are in essence a deviation from this fundamental flight maneuver. Many flight instructors and students are prone to believe that perfection in straight-and-level flight will come of itself, but such is not the case. It is not uncommon to find a pilot whose basic flying ability consistently falls just short of minimum expected standards, and upon analyzing the reasons for the shortcomings to discover that the cause is the inability to fly straight and level properly.

7. Which of these human activities would most closely correlate to straight-and-level flying?

   a. Crawling
   b. Walking
   c. Jogging
   d. Running

Use the passage below to answer the following question:

The National Airspace System (NAS) is the network of United States airspace: air navigation facilities, equipment, services, airports or landing areas, aeronautical charts, information/services, rules, regulations, procedures, technical information, manpower, and material. Included are system components shared jointly with the military. The system's present configuration is a reflection of the technological advances concerning the speed and altitude capability of jet aircraft, as well as the complexity of microchip and satellite-based navigation equipment. To conform to international aviation standards, the United States adopted the primary elements of the classification system developed by the International Civil Aviation Organization (ICAO).

8. Which of these would not be considered part of the National Airspace System?
   a. Airports
   b. Private Flight schools
   c. FAA
   d. Air traffic controllers

Use the passage below to answer the following question:

The effect of free stream density and velocity is a necessary consideration when studying the development of the various aerodynamic forces. Suppose that a particular shape of airfoil is fixed at a particular angle to the airstream. The relative velocity and pressure distribution will be determined by the shape of the airfoil and the angle to the airstream. If the same airfoil shape is placed at the same angle to an airstream with twice as great a dynamic pressure the magnitude of the pressure distribution will be twice as great but the relative shape of the pressure distribution will be the same.

9. Which of these is closest to the meaning of velocity in this passage?
   a. Attitude
   b. Thrust
   c. Speed
   d. Altitude

Use the passage below to answer the following question:

Using a supercharger, at 8,000 feet a typical engine may be able to produce 75 percent of the power it could produce at mean sea level (MSL) because the air is less dense at the higher altitude. The supercharger compresses the air to a higher density allowing a supercharged engine to produce the same manifold pressure at higher altitudes as it could produce at sea level. Thus, an engine at 8,000 feet MSL could still produce 25 "Hg of manifold pressure whereas without a supercharger it could produce only 22 "Hg. Superchargers are especially valuable at high altitudes (such as 18,000 feet) where the air density is 50 percent that of sea level. The use of a supercharger in many cases will supply air to the engine at the same density it did at sea level. With a normally aspirated engine, it is not possible to have manifold pressure higher than the existing atmospheric pressure. A supercharger is capable of boosting manifold pressure above 30 "Hg.

10. According to this passage, if an engine using a supercharger can produce 22 "Hg of manifold pressure at 8,000 feet, approximately how much manifold pressure can it produce at MSL?
   a. 29
   b. 32
   c. 16
   d. 27

Use the passage below to answer the following question:

Learning to manage the many information and automation resources now available to you in the cockpit is a big challenge. Specifically, you must learn how to choose which advanced cockpit systems to use, and when. There are no definitive rules. In fact, you will learn how different features of advanced cockpit avionics systems fall in and out of usefulness depending on the situation. Becoming proficient with advanced avionics means learning to use the right tool for the right job at the right time. In many systems, there are multiple methods of accomplishing the same function. The competent pilot learns all of these methods and chooses the method that works best for the specific situation, environment, and equipment. This handbook will help you get started in learning this important skill.

11. With which of these statements would the author agree?
   a. Choosing an advanced aviation system method is a personal decision best left to each pilot.
   b. Any decent advanced aviation system method will do just fine in most situations.
   c. There is no advanced aviation system method that is a one size fits all solution.
   d. Advanced aviation systems are somewhat overrated.

Use the passage below to answer the following question:

Keeping track of primary flight information is critical at all times, and pilots must become very familiar with their PFD. Flight instrument presentations on a PFD differ from conventional instrumentation not only in format, but sometimes in location as well. Airspeed and altitude indications are presented on vertical tape displays that appear on the left and right sides of the display. The vertical speed indicator is depicted using conventional analog presentation. Turn coordination is shown using a segmented triangle near the top of the attitude indicator. The rate-of-turn indicator appears as a curved line display at the top of the heading/navigation instrument in the lower half of the PFD.

12. In this passage, PFD most likely stands for:
   a. Pilot Flight Details
   b. Power and Features Display
   c. Pilot Flight Display
   d. Primary Flight Display

Use the passage below to answer the following question:

Turbochargers increase the pressure of the engine's induction air, which allows the engine to develop sea level or greater horsepower at higher altitudes. A turbocharger is comprised of two main elements: a compressor and turbine. The compressor section houses an impeller that turns at a high rate of speed. As induction air is drawn across the impeller blades, the impeller accelerates the air, allowing a large volume of air to be drawn into the compressor housing. The impeller's action subsequently produces high-pressure, high-density air, which is delivered to the engine. To turn the impeller, the engine's exhaust gases are used to drive a turbine wheel that is mounted on the opposite end of the impeller's drive shaft. By directing different amounts of exhaust gases to flow over the turbine, more energy can be extracted, causing the impeller to deliver more compressed air to the engine. The waste gate, essentially an adjustable butterfly valve installed in the exhaust system, is used to vary the mass of exhaust gas flowing into the turbine. When closed, most of the exhaust gases from the engine are forced to flow through the turbine. When open, the exhaust gases are allowed to bypass the turbine by flowing directly out through the engine's exhaust pipe.

13. High-density air is delivered to the engine after being produced by the:
   a. Impeller
   b. Inductor
   c. Turbocharger
   d. Butterfly valve

Use the passage below to answer the following two questions:

One of the biggest safety concerns in aviation is the surface movement accident. As a direct result, the Federal Aviation Administration (FAA) has rapidly expanded the information available to pilots, including the addition of taxiway and runway information in FAA publications, particularly the IFR U.S. Terminal Procedures Publication (TPP) booklets and Airport/Facility Directory (A/FD) volumes. The FAA has also implemented new procedures and created educational and awareness programs for pilots, ATC, and ground operators. By focusing resources to attack this problem head on, the FAA hopes to reduce and eventually eliminate surface movement accidents.

Airport sketches and diagrams provide pilots of all levels with graphical depictions of the airport layout. Aeronautical Information Systems (AIS), formerly known as Aeronautical Products (AeroNav), provide an airport sketch on the lower left or right portion of every instrument approach chart. This sketch depicts the runways, their length, width and slope, the touchdown zone elevation, the lighting system installed on the end of the runway, and taxiways. Graphical depictions of NOTAMS are also available for selected airports as well as for temporary flight restriction (TFRs) areas on the defense internet NOTAM service (DINS) website.

For select airports, typically those with heavy traffic or complex runway layouts, AIS also prints an airport diagram. The diagram is located in the IFR TPP booklet following the instrument approach chart for a particular airport. It is a full-page depiction of the airport that includes the same features of the airport sketch plus additional details, such as taxiway identifiers, airport latitude and longitude, and building identification. The airport diagrams are also available in the A/FD and on the AIS website, located at www.aeronav.faa.gov.

14. Which of the following acronyms is not defined by this passage?
   a. TPP
   b. A/FD
   c. NOTAMS
   d. AeroNav

15. Which of the following provides the airport sketches of the airport layout?
   a. AeroNav
   b. AIS
   c. TFR
   d. A/FD

Use the passage below to answer the following question:

Although the regulations specify minimum requirements, the amount of instructional time needed to earn an instrument rating is determined not by the regulation, but by the individual's ability to achieve a satisfactory level of proficiency. A professional pilot with diversified flying experience may easily attain a satisfactory level of proficiency in the minimum time required by regulation. Your own time requirements will depend upon a variety of factors, including previous flying experience, rate of learning, basic ability, frequency of flight training, type of aircraft flown, quality of ground school training, and quality of flight instruction, to name a few. The total instructional time you will need, the scheduling of such time, is up to the individual most qualified to judge your proficiency—the instructor who supervises your progress and endorses your record of flight training.

16. Which of these is not a factor in determining how long it takes a pilot to earn an instrument rating?
   a. Make and model of plane used
   b. Age of pilot
   c. Whether someone is a fast or slow learner
   d. How good the instructor is

Use the passage below to answer the following two questions:

Flight deck crews almost seamlessly launch, recover and deploy aircraft and people all over the flight deck? Did you ever wonder how we do this? Simply put, because we have very dedicated professionals doing their job. However, whether we realize it or not, the success of those individuals who are just "doing their job" hinges upon thorough application of Operational Risk Management on three levels—in depth, when our leadership and acquisition folks provide the equipment, training and guidance for flight deck operations; deliberate, when we plan and brief for the events or operations of the day; and time critical, when we actually apply the risk controls or use the resources provided to us for getting the job done.

17. Which of the following best expresses the meaning of *seamlessly* in this passage?
   a. Without a hitch
   b. Around the clock
   c. Non-stop
   d. Automatically

18 Which of the following is closest in meaning to *deploy*?
   a. Retire from active service
   b. Disguise by using camouflage
   c. Move into position
   d. Recruit or enlist someone into military service

Use the passage below to answer the following question:

Displacing the cyclic forward causes the nose to pitch down initially, with a resultant increase in airspeed and loss of altitude. Aft cyclic causes the nose to pitch up initially, slowing the helicopter and causing it to climb; however, as the helicopter reaches a state of equilibrium, the horizontal stabilizer levels the helicopter airframe to minimize drag, unlike an airplane. Therefore, the helicopter has very little pitch deflection up or down when the helicopter is stable in a flight mode. The variation from absolutely level depends on the particular helicopter and the horizontal stabilizer function. Increasing collective (power) while maintaining a constant airspeed induces a climb while decreasing collective causes a descent. Coordinating these two inputs, down collective plus aft cyclic or up collective plus forward cyclic, results in airspeed changes while maintaining a constant altitude. The pedals serve the same function in both a helicopter and a fixed-wing aircraft, to maintain balanced flight. This is done by applying a pedal input in whichever direction is necessary to center the ball in the turn and bank indicator.

19. According to this article, what is one of the main factors when it comes to variation from absolute level?
   a. The horizontal stabilizer
   b. The direction of the wind
   c. The speed of the wind
   d. Whether the weight of passengers and cargo is properly balanced

Use the passage below to answer the following question:

Making good choices sounds easy enough. However, there are a multitude of factors that come into play when these choices, and subsequent decisions, are made in the aeronautical world. Many tools are available for pilots to become more self-aware and assess the options available, along with the impact of their decision. Yet, with all the available resources, accident rates are not being reduced. Poor decisions continue to be made, frequently resulting in lives being lost and/or aircraft damaged or destroyed. The Risk Management Handbook discusses aeronautical decision-making (ADM) and single-pilot resource management (SRM) in detail and should be thoroughly read and understood. While progress is continually being made in the advancement of pilot training methods, aircraft equipment and systems, and services for pilots, accidents still occur. Historically, the term "pilot error" has been used to describe the causes of these accidents. Pilot error means an action or decision made by the pilot was the cause of, or a contributing factor that led to, the accident. This definition also includes the pilot's failure to make a decision or take action. From a broader perspective, the phrase "human factors related" more aptly describes these accidents since it is usually not a single decision that leads to an accident, but a chain of events triggered by a number of factors. The poor judgment chain, sometimes referred to as the "error chain," is a term used to describe this concept of contributing factors in a human factors related accident.

123

Breaking one link in the chain is often the only event necessary to change the outcome of the sequence of events.

20. Which of the following statements would the author be most likely to agree with?
   a. The problem of aircraft accidents has never been worse.
   b. Realistically, the number of aircraft accidents is probably as low as it's ever going to be.
   c. There is still much room for improvement when it comes to reducing aircraft accidents.
   d. Great strides have been made in recent years in reducing the number of aircraft accidents.

Use the passage below to answer the following question:

When an operator requests a Minimum Equipment List (MEL), and a Letter of Authorization (LOA) is issued by the FAA, then the use of the MEL becomes mandatory for that helicopter. All maintenance deferrals must be accomplished in accordance with the terms and conditions of the MEL and the operator-generated procedures document. Exercise extreme caution when hovering near buildings or other aircraft. The use of an MEL for rotorcraft operated under part 91 also allows for the deferral of inoperative items or equipment. The primary guidance becomes the FAA-approved MEL issued to that specific operator and N-numbered helicopter. The FAA has developed master minimum equipment lists (MMELs) for rotorcraft in current use. Upon written request by a rotorcraft operator, the local FAA Flight Standards District Office (FSDO) may issue the appropriate make and model MMEL, along with an LOA, and the preamble. The operator then develops operations and maintenance (O&M) procedures from the MMEL. This MMEL with O&M procedures now becomes the operator's MEL. The MEL, LOA, preamble, and procedures document developed by the operator must be on board the helicopter when it is operated. The FAA considers an approved MEL to be a supplemental type certificate (STC) issued to an aircraft by serial number and registration number. It therefore becomes the authority to operate that aircraft in a condition other than originally type certificated. With an approved MEL, if the position lights were discovered inoperative prior to a daytime flight, the pilot would make an entry in the maintenance record or discrepancy record provided for that purpose. The item is then either repaired or deferred in accordance with the MEL. Upon confirming that daytime flight with inoperative position lights is acceptable in accordance with the provisions of the MEL, the pilot would leave the position lights switch OFF, open the circuit breaker (or whatever action is called for in the procedures document), and placard the position light switch as INOPERATIVE.

21. What resource would a pilot use to determine if an inoperative part or system rendered daytime flight unacceptable?
   a. LOA
   b. O&M
   c. FSDO
   d. MEL

Use the passage below to answer the following question:

It is important to understand the three levels of Operational Risk Management, because each level plays a role in improving our chance of completing the mission successfully. In particular, the controls developed at each level are resources we can tap into to accomplish our job or mission during its execution. These resources make it easier to do our job and help catch errors that might be detrimental to task or mission success. Beyond the equipment itself and our fellow shipmates, there are other resources we can tap to help mitigate the risks associated with the hazards of the flight deck.

22. Which of the following is closest in meaning to mitigate?
   a. Eliminate
   b. Control
   c. Reduce
   d. Understand

Use the passage below to answer the following question:

Today, helicopters are quite reliable. However, emergencies do occur, whether as a result of mechanical failure or pilot error, and should be anticipated. Regardless of the cause, the recovery needs to be quick and precise. By having a thorough knowledge of the helicopter and its systems, a pilot is able to handle the situation more readily. Helicopter emergencies and the proper recovery procedures should be discussed and, when possible, practiced in flight. In addition, by knowing the conditions that can lead to an emergency, many potential accidents can be avoided. Emergencies should always be anticipated. Knowledge of the helicopter, possible malfunctions and failures, and methods of recovery can help the pilot avoid accidents and be a safer pilot. Helicopter pilots should always expect the worst hazards and possible aerodynamic effects and plan for a safe exit path or procedure to compensate for the hazard.

23. Which of the following best sums up this passage?
   a. Planning ahead is the best way to prepare for emergencies.
   b. Many helicopter emergencies are due to faulty equipment.
   c. In helicopter emergencies, there is little margin for error.
   d. Helicopter emergencies can arise at any time and for a variety of reasons.

Use the passage below to answer the following question:

Medium-frequency vibrations (1,000–2,000 cycles per minute) range between the low frequencies of the main rotor (100–500 cycles per minute) and the high frequencies (2,100 cycles per minute or higher) of the engine and tail rotor. Depending on the helicopter, medium-frequency vibration sources may be engine and transmission cooling fans, and accessories such as air conditioner compressors, or driveline components. Medium-frequency vibrations are felt through the entire airframe, and prolonged exposure to the vibrations will result in greater pilot fatigue. Most tail rotor vibrations fall into the high-frequency range (2,100 cycles per minute or higher) and can be felt through the tail rotor pedals as long as there are no hydraulic actuators to dampen out the vibration. This vibration is felt by the pilot through his or her feet, which are usually "put to sleep" by the vibration. The tail rotor operates at approximately a 6:1 ratio with the main rotor, meaning for every one rotation of the main rotor the tail rotor rotates 6 times. A main rotor operating rpm of 350 means the tail rotor rpm would be 2,100 rpm. Any imbalance in the tail rotor system is very harmful as it can cause cracks to develop and rivets to work loose. Piston engines usually produce a normal amount of high-frequency vibration, which is aggravated by engine malfunctions, such as spark plug fouling, incorrect magneto timing, carburetor icing and/or incorrect fuel/air mixture. Vibrations in turbine engines are often difficult to detect as these engines operate at a very high rpm. Turbine engine vibration can be at 30,000 rpm internally, but common gearbox speeds are in the 1,000 to 3,000 rpm range for the output shaft. The vibrations in turbine engines may be short lived as the engine disintegrates rapidly when damaged due to high rpm and the forces present.

24. Which frequencies can result in the pilot experiencing numbness in the pilot's leg?
   a. Low frequency vibrations
   b. Medium frequency vibrations
   c. High frequency vibrations
   d. Both medium and high frequency vibrations

Use the passage below to answer the following question:

Rigid rotor systems tend to behave like fully articulated systems through aerodynamics, but lack flapping or lead/ lag hinges. Instead, the blades accommodate these motions by bending. They cannot flap or lead/lag but they can be feathered. As advancements in helicopter aerodynamics and materials continue to improve, rigid rotor systems may become more common because the system is fundamentally easier to design and offers the best properties of both semirigid and fully articulated systems. The rigid rotor system is very responsive and is usually not susceptible to mast bumping like the semirigid or articulated systems because the rotor hubs are mounted solid to the main rotor mast. This allows the rotor and fuselage to move together as one entity and eliminates much of the oscillation usually present in the other rotor systems. Other advantages of the rigid rotor include a reduction in the weight and drag of the rotor hub and a larger flapping arm, which significantly reduces control inputs. Without the complex hinges, the rotor system becomes much more reliable and easier to maintain than the other rotor configurations. A disadvantage of this system is the quality of ride in turbulent or gusty air. Because there are no hinges to help absorb the larger loads, vibrations are felt in the cabin much more than with other rotor head designs. There are several variations of the basic three rotor head designs. The bearingless rotor system is closely related to the articulated rotor system, but has no bearings or hinges. This design relies on the structure of blades and hub to absorb stresses. The main difference between the rigid rotor system and the bearingless system is that the bearingless system has no feathering bearing—the material inside the cuff is twisted by the action of the pitch change arm. Nearly all bearingless rotor hubs are made of fiber-composite materials.

25. The author of this passage would probably agree most strongly with which statement about rigid rotor systems?
   a. They are less popular than they used to be.
   b. They result in fewer vibrations than semirigid and fully articulated systems.
   c. Overall, they're superior to semirigid and fully articulated systems.
   d. They are not as safe as semirigid and fully articulated systems.

Use the passage below to answer the following question:

The roots of aviation are firmly based on curiosity. Where would we be today had it not been for the dreams of Leonardo da Vinci, the Wright Brothers, and Igor Sikorsky? They all were infatuated with flight, a curiosity that led to the origins of aviation. The tale of aviation is full of firsts: first flight, first helicopter, first trans-Atlantic flight, and so on. But, along the way there were many setbacks, fatalities, and lessons learned. Today, we continue to learn and investigate the limits of aviation. We've been to the moon, and soon beyond. Our curiosity will continue to drive us to search for the next challenge. However, curiosity can also have catastrophic consequences. Despite over 100 years of aviation practice, we still see accidents that are caused by impaired judgment formed from curious behavior. Pilots commonly seek to determine the limits of their ability as well as the limits of the aircraft. Unfortunately, too often this leads to mishaps with deadly results. Inquisitive behavior must be harnessed and displayed within personal and material limits. Deadly curiosity may not seem as obvious to some as it is to others. Simple thoughts such as, "Is visibility really as bad as what the ATIS is reporting?" or "Does the 20-minute fuel light really indicate only 20 minutes' worth of fuel?" can lead to poor decisions and disastrous outcomes. Some aviators blatantly violate rules and aircraft limitations without thinking through the consequences. "What indications and change in flight characteristics will I see if I fly this helicopter above its maximum gross weight?" or "I've heard this helicopter can do aerobatic flight. Why is it prohibited?" are examples of extremely harmful curiosity. Even more astounding is their ignoring the fact that the damage potentially done to the aircraft will probably manifest later in the aircraft's life, affecting other crews. Spontaneous excursions in aviation can be deadly. Curiosity is natural, and promotes learning. Airmen should abide by established procedures until proper and complete hazard assessment and risk management can be completed.

26. Which of these statements most closely matches the theme of this passage?
   a. Fortune favors the bold.
   b. An ounce of prevention is worth a pound of cure.
   c. Curiosity killed the cat.
   d. Fools rush in where angels fear to tread.

Use the passage below to answer the following question:

Although helicopters were developed and built during the first half-century of flight, some even reaching limited production; it was not until 1942 that a helicopter designed by Igor Sikorsky reached full-scale production, with 131 aircraft built. Even though most previous designs used more than one main rotor, it was the single main rotor with an antitorque tail rotor configuration design that would come to be recognized worldwide as the helicopter. In 1951, at the urging of his contacts at the Department of the Navy, Charles H. Kaman modified his K-225 helicopter with a new kind of engine, the turbo-shaft engine. This adaptation of the turbine engine provided a large amount of horsepower to the helicopter with a lower weight penalty than piston engines, heavy engine blocks, and auxiliary components. On December 11, 1951, the K-225 became the first turbine-powered helicopter in the world. Two years later, on March 26, 1954, a modified Navy HTK-1, another Kaman helicopter, became the first twin-turbine helicopter to fly. However, it was the Sud Aviation Alouette II that would become the first helicopter to be produced with a turbine engine. Reliable helicopters capable of stable hover flight were developed decades after fixed-wing aircraft. This is largely due to higher engine power density requirements than fixed-wing aircraft. Improvements in fuels and engines during the first half of the 20th century were a critical factor in helicopter development. The availability of lightweight turbo-shaft engines in the second half of the 20th century led to the development of larger, faster, and higher-performance helicopters. The turbine engine has the following advantages over a reciprocating engine: less vibration, increased aircraft performance, reliability, and ease of operation. While smaller and less expensive helicopters still use piston engines, turboshaft engines are the preferred powerplant for helicopters today.

27. Which of these is most responsible for a huge increase in the variety of helicopters in use?
   a. The military demand for helicopters in World War II
   b. The development of an antitorque tail rotor configuration design
   c. The development of turbine engine powered helicopters
   d. The development of piston engine helicopters

Mechanical Comprehension Test

1. A cannon fires off a ship up towards a mountain range. Neglecting air resistance, where will the velocity of the projectile be greatest?

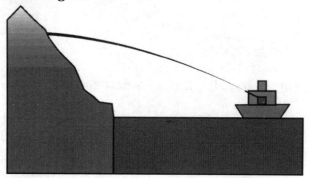

    a.   Exiting the muzzle
    b.   Halfway to the mountains
    c.   As it impacts the mountains

2. These pulleys are connected by belts. Which pulley travels the fastest?

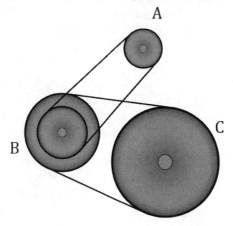

    a.   Pulley A
    b.   Pulley B
    c.   Pulley C

3. If Gear A is traveling at 10 rpm, how many times will Gear C rotate in 3 minutes?

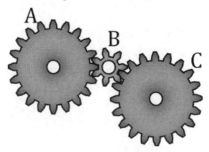

    a.   1.7 times
    b.   3 times
    c.   30 times

4. Where should the fulcrum be located to balance this beam?

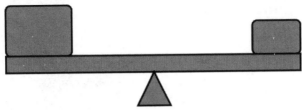

    a.   closer to the large mass
    b.   closer to the small mass
    c.   exactly between the two masses

5. Which orientation will require more force to pull?

    a.   with the rope at an angle to the table
    b.   with the rope parallel to the table
    c.   both orientations are equal

6. The larger piston has four times as much horizontal area as the smaller piston. If the small piston is compressed 8 inches, how far will the larger piston move?

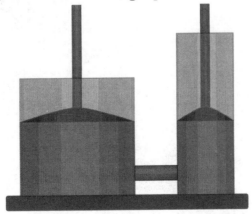

    a.   8 inches
    b.   2 inches
    c.   32 inches

7. A wing in flight has a set of pressures causing the overall forces on the top and bottom of the wing. Where will the total force on the wing point?

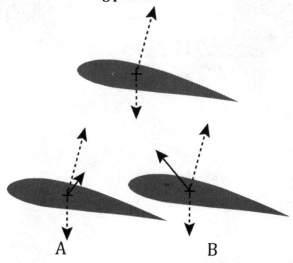

a. up and to the right
b. up and to the left
c. neither A or B

8. River water enters a section where the water spreads out into a wide, deep area. Is the water likely to speed up, slow down, or remain at a constant speed?

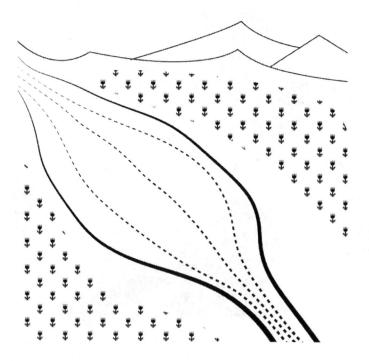

a. speed up
b. slow down
c. remain at a constant speed

9. A magnet is placed in the middle of two identical, anchored magnets. Which direction will the magnet go?

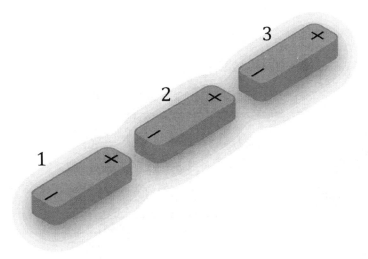

    a.   towards magnet 1
    b.   towards magnet 2
    c.   the magnet won't move

10. A solid substance melts at -21°C. If the object is known to change phase at 81°C, will the object be a solid, liquid, or gas at 90°C?

    a.   solid
    b.   liquid
    c.   gas

11. If the resistors in the circuits are identical, which circuit will have the greatest overall resistance?

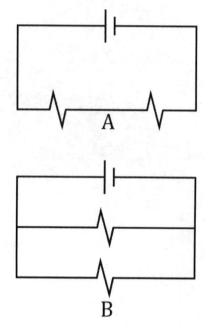

a. circuit A
b. circuit B
c. circuit A and B have the same overall resistance

12. A pendulum swings back and forth once per second. The pendulum is shortened by removing half of the string. The new frequency is 1.4 Hz (Hz=1/sec). How often will the pendulum swing back and forth in a minute?

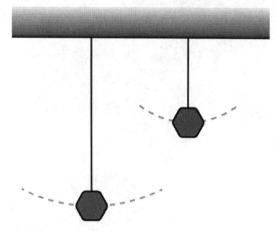

a. 84
b. 92
c. 72

13. Two identical pistons are connected by a pipe. What is the mechanical advantage of the piston system?

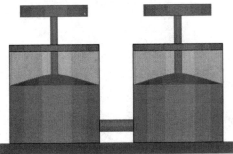

   a. 0.5
   b. 1
   c. 2

14. A ball is thrown horizontally off a cliff at the same time that an identical ball is dropped off a cliff. How long after the dropped ball hits the ground will the thrown ball hit?

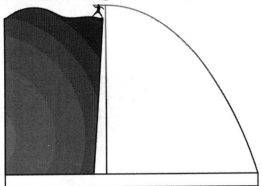

   a. approximately 1 second after
   b. approximately 2 seconds after
   c. they will hit at the same time

15. The cam rotates at 5 rpm. How many times will the follower (needle) move up and down in a minute?

    a. 20
    b. 72
    c. 140

16. Which of the following are not ways to increase the torque applied to a wrench?

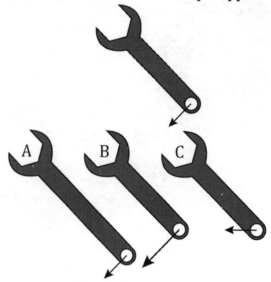

    a. increase the length from the center to the applied force
    b. increase the force
    c. angle the force toward the center

17. A ball is pushed down into a vertical spring. The ball is released and flies upward. Which best describes the states of energy the ball underwent?

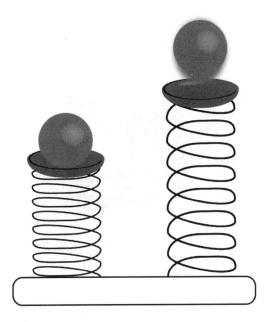

   a. convective energy to potential energy
   b. potential energy to kinetic energy
   c. kinetic energy to potential energy

18. A vacuum tank is held by weights at a depth of 50 feet underwater. If the tank is raised to a depth of 25 feet, will the pressure on the walls of the tank increase, decrease, or stay the same?

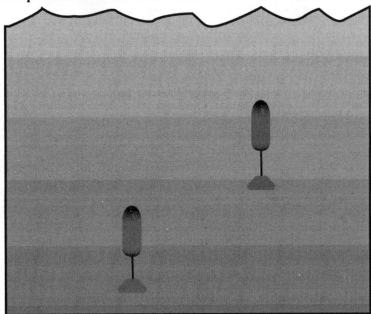

   a. increase
   b. decrease
   c. stay the same

19. Adding salt to water raises its density. Will salt water have a lower, higher, or the same specific gravity than 1?

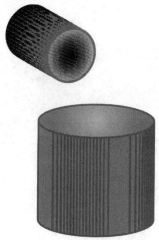

a. lower
b. higher
c. the same

20. Which of the following is an example of convective heat transfer?

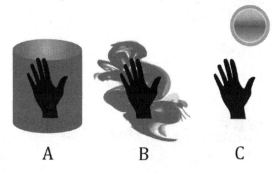

A   B   C

a. a man burns his hand on a hot pot
b. a man burns his hand in steam
c. a man gets a sun burn

21. Which of the following is the electrical component which holds a voltage across a gap between two conductive materials?

a. resistor
b. inductor
c. capacitor

22. **Which of these wrenches is likely to provide the greatest torque with a set force?**

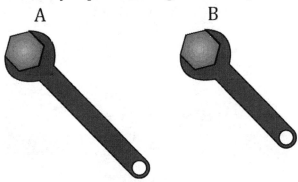

     A   B

    a.   wrench A
    b.   wrench B
    c.   both wrenches will provide the same torque

23. **Which of the following is true of this circuit?**

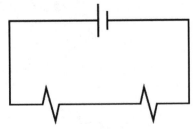

    a.   the voltage is the same everywhere
    b.   the current is the same everywhere
    c.   there is no current

24. **Which device does not measure current in an electrical system?**

    a.   ammeter
    b.   multimeter
    c.   voltmeter

25. A ball is thrown straight into the air with an initial kinetic energy of 100 ft-lb. What is the potential energy of the ball at half of the height of the flight path?

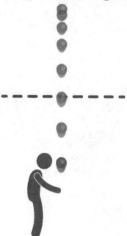

    a.   33 ft-lb
    b.   50 ft-lb
    c.   66 ft-lb

26. An increase in mechanical advantage with a set motion for the load and a set applied force necessitates an increase in _____ the applied force?

    a.   the distance traveled by
    b.   the angle of action of
    c.   the potential energy behind

27. A windlass drum has two sections with different circumferences. When winding the drum, one side of the rope winds around the large section and the other unwinds from the small section. If the large section of the drum has a circumference of 3.5 ft and the other section has a circumference of 1 ft, how far will the weight lift with two full turns of the drum?

    a.   2.5 feet
    b.   9 feet
    c.   4.5 feet

28. Which type of situation will lead to condensation on the outside of pipes?

    a. hot liquid in the pipe and cold air outside the pipe
    b. cold liquid in the pipe and colder air outside the pipe
    c. cold liquid in the pipe and hot air outside the pipe

29. Which color will absorb the most radiation?

    a. black
    b. green
    c. dark yellow

30. Two gears (30 and 18 teeth) mesh. If the smaller gear rotates 3 times, how many times will the larger gear rotate?

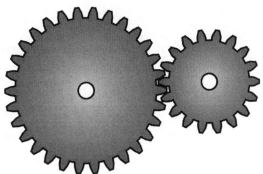

    a. 1.6 times
    b. 1.8 times
    c. 3 times

Aviation and Nautical Information Test

1. What would be the name of a runway that the pilot approaches while heading due east?

    a. Runway 01
    b. Runway 09
    c. Runway 27
    d. Runway E
    e. Runway B

2. Which part of a fixed-wing airplane supplies the thrust?

    a. tail assembly
    b. control surfaces
    c. fuselage
    d. landing gear
    e. powerplant

3. What is the path of the chord line on a wing?

    a. from leading edge to trailing edge, through the wing
    b. from leading edge to trailing edge, along the surface of the wing
    c. along the inside of the wing, such that the upper and lower wings are equal in thickness
    d. from one wingtip to the other
    e. from wingtip to fuselage

4. Which of the following statements about a medium bank is true?

    a. A plane will tend to level out from a medium bank unless there is input from the pilot.
    b. A plane that is put into a medium bank will tend to increase its bank unless the ailerons are applied.
    c. A medium bank is between ten and thirty degrees.
    d. A medium bank is between thirty and fifty degrees.
    e. A plane will tend to remain in a medium bank until the pilot makes an adjustment.

5. Which of the following is NOT one of the four basic maneuvers in flight?

    a. turn
    b. spin
    c. straight-and-level flight
    d. climb
    e. descent

6. The introduction of which of the following was the main breakthrough that led to the widespread use of jets on aircraft carriers?

    a. Optical landing system
    b. Ski-jump ramp
    c. Steam-powered catapult
    d. Hydraulic catapult
    e. Angled flight deck

7. From approximately how far away should a Visual Approach Slope Indicator be visible at night?

   a. Five miles
   b. Ten miles
   c. Twenty miles
   d. Thirty miles
   e. Fifty miles

8. Which of the following is NOT one of the forces a pilot must manage during flight?

   a. thrust
   b. gravity
   c. drag
   d. lift
   e. torque

9. Which control affects the angle of the main rotor blades of a helicopter?

   a. collective
   b. throttle
   c. cyclic
   d. directional control system
   e. None of the above

10. Who was the first man to successfully land a plane on a moving ship?

   a. Orville Wright
   b. Thomas Schumacher
   c. William Hart
   d. Edwin Dunning
   e. Robert Lundquist

11. What is the flight attitude?

   a. the environment immediately around the plane
   b. the morale of the flight crew
   c. the position of the plane in motion
   d. the inclination of the elevators
   e. the positions of the ailerons

12. The curvature of an airfoil is known as the

   a. bank.
   b. position.
   c. camber.
   d. angle.
   e. attitude.

13. Which of the following is considered one of the primary flight controls?

   a. elevators
   b. leading edge devices
   c. flaps
   d. spoilers
   e. trim tabs

14. What is the term in aviation for movement around the plane's longitudinal axis?

a. stalling
b. rolling
c. pitching
d. leaning
e. yawing

15. Which of these is NOT one of the sets of lights that make up an optical landing system?

a. Wave-off
b. Datum
c. Ball
d. Power-up
e. Cut

16. Which country built the first ship deliberately designed as an aircraft carrier?

a. Japan
b. USSR
c. England
d. United States
e. Canada

17. The vertical axis of a plane extends upward through the plane's

a. cockpit.
b. tail.
c. landing gear.
d. center of mass.
e. geometric center.

18. When is trimming necessary?

a. when the plane is ascending or descending
b. after the elevators have been deflected upwards
c. after the ailerons have been adjusted
d. after the elevators have been deflected downwards
e. after any change in the flight condition

19. How far away is an approaching plane when the Runway Centerline Lighting System lights become solid red?

a. Five hundred feet
b. One thousand feet
c. Three thousand feet
d. Five thousand feet
e. One mile

20. **What is the Coriolis force?**
    a. the extra lift generated by a helicopter once it has exited its own downwash
    b. the force that spins the rotors of a helicopter even when there is no power from the engine
    c. the greater downwash at the rear half of the rotor disc, as compared with the front
    d. the phenomenon in which the effects of a force applied to a spinning disc occur ninety degrees later
    e. the change in rotational speed caused by the shift of the weight towards or away from the center of the spinning object

21. **What is the primary determinant of air pressure in the flight envelope?**
    a. the altitude at which the plane is flying
    b. the camber of the wings
    c. the amount of lift that the airfoils can create
    d. the pitch of the elevators
    e. the humidity of the air

22. **A plane is said to have conventional landing gear when the third wheel is**
    a. aligned with the second wheel.
    b. under the tail.
    c. directly behind the first wheel.
    d. under the nose.
    e. underneath the cockpit.

23. **Which of the following was America's first nuclear-powered aircraft carrier?**
    a. USS Princeton
    b. USS Enterprise
    c. USS Langley
    d. USS Kitty Hawk
    e. USS Constellation

24. **Who was the first person to fly an aircraft from a moving ship?**
    a. Arthur Harrison
    b. Charles Samson
    c. Reginald Jackson
    d. Maurice Farman
    e. Eugene Ely

25. **Which of the following is NOT part of the empennage?**
    a. rudder
    b. trim tab
    c. elevator
    d. aileron
    e. horizontal stabilizer

26. A glider would be most likely to have a

    a.   delta wing.
    b.   triangular wing.
    c.   forward swept wing.
    d.   backward swept wing.
    e.   straight wing.

27. Which of the following is NOT considered part of a plane's basic weight?

    a.   crew
    b.   fuel
    c.   external equipment
    d.   internal equipment
    e.   fuselage

28. The support structure that runs the length of the fuselage in a monocoque plane is called a

    a.   counter.
    b.   former.
    c.   truss.
    d.   stringer.
    e.   bulkhead.

29. Which control is used to manipulate the elevators on an airplane?

    a.   throttle
    b.   rudder
    c.   joystick
    d.   pedals
    e.   collective

30. Which maneuver is appropriate when a pilot needs to descend quickly onto a shorter-than-normal runway?

    a.   descent at minimum safe airspeed
    b.   idle
    c.   partial power descent
    d.   glide
    e.   stall

Answer Key and Explanations

Math Skills Test

1. A: First, subtract 4 from both sides to isolate x:

$16x + 4 - 4 = 100 - 4$

$16x = 96$

Then, divide both sides by 16 to solve for x:

$16x/16 = 96/16$

$x = 6$

2. A: Use the FOIL method (first, outside, inside, and last) to get rid of the brackets:

$10x^2 + 20x - 100x - 200$

Then, combine like terms to simplify the expression:

$10x^2 - 80x - 200$

3. A: Complementary angles are two angles that equal 90° when added together.

4. D: To simplify this expression, the law of exponents that states that $(x^m)^n = x^{m*n}$ must be observed:

$2^3 x^{4*3} + 2 (y^{5*5})$

$8x^{12} + 2y^{25}$

5. A: The sum of the measures of the three angles of any triangle is 180. The equation of the angles of this triangle can be written as $2x + 6x + 10x = 180$, or $18x = 180$. Therefore, x = 10. Therefore, the measure of the smallest angle is 20.

6. B: The formula for the area of a circle is πr^2. The diameter of a circle is equal to twice its radius. Therefore, to find the radius of this circle, it is necessary to divide the diameter by 2: 12 / 2 = 6cm

Then, use the formula to find the area of the circle: $\pi 6^2$

$\pi * 36 = 113 cm^2$

7. D: The general equation to find the area of a quadrilateral is length * width.

Since the length and width of a square are equal, we can calculate the area of the square described in the question:

$A = l * w$

$A = 15cm * 15cm$

$A = 225 cm^2$

145

8. C: To find the volume of a rectangular solid, the formula is length * width * height.

Therefore, this solid's volume = 12cm * 3cm * 9cm = 324cm³

9. C: First, add $4x^2$ to both sides to isolate x:

$2x^2 + 4x^2 = -4x^2 + 4x^2 + 216$

$6x^2 = 216$

Then, divide both sides by 6:

$6x^2/6 = 216/6$

$x^2 = 36$

Finally, take the square root of both sides to solve for x:

$\sqrt{x^2} = \sqrt{36}$

$x = 6$

10. B: The general equation to find the area of a quadrilateral is length * width.

Since the length and width of a square are equal, we can calculate the area of the square described in the question. We can divide the perimeter by 4 since all sides are equal length. Once we know each side is 6 m we can multiply 6*6 to get an area of 36 m^2.

11. B: The formula for the area of a rectangle is length * width. Using the measurements given in the question, the area of the rectangle can be calculated:

A = length * width

A = 5cm * 7cm

A = 35cm²

12. B: On a six-sided die, the probability of throwing any number is 1 in 6. The probability of throwing a 3 or a 4 is double that, or 2 in 6. This can be simplified by dividing both 2 and 6 by 2.

Therefore, the probability of throwing either a 3 or 4 is 1 in 3.

13. C: First, add the 24 and the 6:

-2y ≥ 30

Then, divide both sides by -2 to solve for y:

-2y/-2 ≥ 30/-2

y ≥ -15

Finally, when both sides are divided by a negative number, the direction of the sign must be reversed:

y ≤ -15

14. A: First, bring the 5x to the left side of the equation to make it easier to solve:

2x – 5x = -30

-3x = -30

Then, divide both sides by -3 to solve for x:

-3x/-3 = -30/-3

x = 10

15. C: The solution of $f(x) = g(x)$ can be determined by setting the two functions equal to one another. Thus, the following may be written $3x + 6 = 2x - 8$. Solving for x gives $x = -14$.

16. A: The area of a square is equal to the square of the length of one side. If the area is 64 in², the side length must therefore be $\sqrt{64\text{in}^2} = 8$ in. The circle is inscribed in the square, so the side length of the square is the same as the circle's diameter. If the circle's diameter is 8 in, then the circle's radius must be half of that, or 4 in. The area of a circle is equal to $A = \pi r^2 = \pi(4 \text{ in})^2 = 16\pi \text{ in}^2$.

17. A: First, bring the -3x to the left side of the equation and the 23 to the right side of the equation to make it easier to solve:

4x + 3x > -6 – 23

7x > -29

Then, divide both side by 7 to solve for x:

7x/7> -29/7

x > -4.14

18. D: First, bring all of the terms containing x to the left side of the equation to make it easier to solve: 2x + 5x – 3x – x = 30

7x – 4x = 30

3x = 30

Then, divide both sides by 3 to solve for x:

3x/3 = 30/3

x=10

19. B: First, substitute the given values for x and y into the expression:

3(4)² 10 + 10/2 – 6(4)

Then, calculate the value of the expression:

According to the order of operations, any multiplying and dividing must be done first:

3*16*10 + 5 – 24

480 + 5 − 24

Then, any addition or subtraction should be completed:

485 − 24

461

20. B: The average is the total amount spent divided by the number of students. The first three students spend an average of $10, so the total amount they spend is 3 × $10 = $30. The other six students spend an average of $4, so the total amount they spend is 6 × $4 = $24. The total amount spent by all nine students is $30 + $24 = $54, and the average amount they spend is $54 ÷ 9 = $6.

21. C: First, substitute the given value of w (7) into the expression each time it appears.

$8*7^2 − 12(7) + (4*7 − 5) + 6$

According to the order of operations, any calculations inside of the brackets must be done first:

$8*7^2 − 12(7) + (23) + 6$

Finally, calculate the value of the expression:

8*49 − 84 + 23 + 6

392 − 84 + 23 + 6

337

22. C: First, subtract 7 from both sides to isolate x:

x/3 + 7 − 7 = 35 − 7

x/3 = 28

Then, multiply both sides by three to solve for x:

x/3 * 3 = 28 * 3

x = 84

23. B: First, bring all terms to the left side of the equation to make it easier to solve:

$2x^2 -7x - x^2 +12 = 0$

Combine like terms:

$x^2 -7x + 12 = 0$

Then, factor the equation:

(x − 4) (x − 3) =0

Finally, solve for x in both instances:

x − 4 = 0

x = 4

x – 3 = 0

x = 3

x = 3, 4

24. A: Another way of expressing the fact that x is 25% of 250 is:

x = (0.25)250

Then, it is simply a matter of multiplying out the right side of the equation to calculate the value of x: x = 62.5

25. B: The volume of a cube is calculated by cubing the length, width, or height of the cube (the value for all three of these is the same.

Therefore, the volume of a cube equals = length³

In this case 8cm³= x * x * x, where x can represent the length of the cube.

To find the length, we must figure out which number cubed equals 8.

The answer is 2cm: 2cm * 2cm * 2cm = 8cm³

26. B: One way to compare fractions is to convert them to equivalent fractions which have common denominators. In this case the lowest common denominator of the three fractions is $7 \times 12 = 84$. Converting each of the fractions to this denominator, $\frac{1}{3} = \frac{1 \times 28}{3 \times 28} = \frac{28}{84}, \frac{2}{7} = \frac{2 \times 12}{7 \times 12} = \frac{24}{84}$, and $\frac{5}{12} = \frac{5 \times 7}{12 \times 7} = \frac{35}{84}$. Since $24 < 28 < 35$, it must be the case that $\frac{2}{7} < \frac{1}{3} < \frac{5}{12}$.

27. A: Use the FOIL (first, outside, inside, last) to expand the expression:

4x³ -2x² +6x – 3

There are no like terms, so the expression cannot be simplified any further.

28. D: To simplify this expression, the law of exponents that states that $x^m * x^n = x^{m+n}$ must be observed.

10x⁴⁺²y⁷⁺³m²⁺⁸z

Therefore, 10x⁶y¹⁰m¹⁰z is the simplified expression.

29. C: First, find the total number of students in the classroom: 13 + 18 = 31

There is an 18 in 31 chance that a name chosen randomly will be a girl's name.

To express this as a percentage, divide 18 by 31, then multiply that number by 100:

18/31 * 100% = 58%

30. A: *x* percent is the same thing as $\frac{x}{100}$, and finding *x* percent of a number is the same as multiplying that number by *x* percent. This is true even when the number is itself a percent. So, 10% of 40% is 40% × 10% = 40% × $\frac{10}{100}$ = 40% × $\frac{1}{10}$ = 4%.

Reading Comprehension Test

1. D: Battery and ignition switches: Off

Control column locks: Removed

Landing gear control: Down and locked

Airspeed Indicator needle: 0

2. B: The primer is a small pump used to draw fuel from the tanks to vaporize it directly into the cylinders prior to starting the engine.

3. D: While the article does state that radial engines were widely used during WW II, it doesn't say how much use in-line engines got.

4. B: Harrowing means extremely disturbing

5. C: 75 degrees Fahrenheit and 60% relative humidity

6. B: 60 degrees Fahrenheit and 85% relative humidity

7. B: Walking is the fundamental way of moving for a mature human being, and jogging and running are deviations of walking, just as straight-and-level flying is the fundamental flight maneuver, and all other flight maneuvers are considered to be deviations of it.

8. B: Flight schools not affiliated with the government or the military would not be considered part of the National Airspace System. They might conduct some of their training at airports, which are part of the NAS, but the school itself would not be considered an NAS component.

9. C: Of the four answer choices, *Speed* is the closest in meaning to *velocity*.

10. A: 29. Using a supercharger, at 8,000 feet a typical engine may be able to produce 75 percent of the power it could produce at mean sea level (MSL) because the air is less dense at the higher altitude. So, if it can produce 22 "Hg at 8,000 feet, that represents 75% of its potential production at MSL. Dividing 22 by .75 gives us 29.333.

11. C: The author makes it clear that there is no advanced aviation system method that works best in every situation, and pilots need to choose the right method based on the circumstances.

12. D: Primary Flight Display. From the context, we know that PFD most likely refers to both *primary* and *display*, and D is the only answer choice that contains both words.

13. A: Impeller. The passage states that the impeller's action produces high-pressure, high-density air, which is then delivered to the engine.

14. C: NOTAMS is used in the passage, but isn't defined. It stands for Notices to Airmen. The singular is NOTAM, for Notice to Airmen. A NOTAM is a notification to pilots of factors along a flight path or at a destination that could be hazardous.

15. B: AIS stands for Aeronautical Information Systems, which is a division of the Federal Aviation Administration.

16. B: Although the passage states that how much experience a pilot has is important, the age of the pilot is not listed as a factor in how quickly one can earn an instrument rating. All of the other answer choices are listed in the passage as factors, although not in the same exact words.

17. A: *Seamlessly* in this context means *easily and without interruptions*, and *without a hitch* is another way of expressing that.

18. C: Of the four answer choices, *move into position* best expresses the meaning of *deploy*.

19. A: The passages states: "The variation from absolutely level depends on the particular helicopter and the horizontal stabilizer function."

20. C: This statement is the only one backed up by the contents of the passage.

21. D: The Minimum Equipment List (MEL) is the correct answer, based on this part of the passage: The FAA considers an approved MEL to be a supplemental type certificate (STC) issued to an aircraft by serial number and registration number. It therefore becomes the authority to operate that aircraft in a condition other than originally type certificated.

22. C: *Reduce* and *mitigate* have almost the same meaning.

23. A: The author's main point in this passage is that pilots can best prepare for emergencies by planning ahead – taking the time to master the helicopter and its systems, and anticipating emergencies and how to respond to them before they happen.

24. C: The passage states that high frequency vibrations can cause numbness in the pilot's leg.

25. C: The author says that rigid rotor systems offer the best properties of semirigid and fully articulated systems, and are easier to design, too.

26. D: Fools rush in where angels fear to tread expresses the idea that people who are new or inexperienced at something will often take dangerous chances that wiser or more experienced people would steer clear of, which most closely matches the author's theme that unbridled curiosity in a pilot can lead to disaster. He is not saying curiosity is bad in and of itself; only that it needs to have limits. That's why *Curiosity killed the cat* is incorrect.

27. C: Taking the entire passage as a whole, it shows that the development of turbine engine powered helicopters is the factor that was most responsible for a huge increase in the variety of helicopters in use.

Mechanical Comprehension Test

1. A: The velocity is made up of two components, the x and y components. The x component is not changing during flight, but the weight of the projectile decreases the positive y component of the velocity. Thus, the total velocity will be greatest before the y component has decreased.

2. A: Because the linear speed of two connected pulleys is the same, the pulley with the smaller radius spins faster. The largest pulley will spin slower than the middle pulley. The smallest pulley will spin faster than the middle pulley, making it the fastest pulley.

3. C: Gear A and gear C have the same number of teeth. Thus, gears A and C will have the same speed. Since gear C is rotating at 10 rpm, the total number of rotations is calculated by multiplying the rpm by the number of minutes.

4. A: Because the large mass will produce a greater torque at the same distance from the fulcrum as the small mass, the distance from the large mass to the fulcrum should be shortened. Then, the torque produced by the large mass will decrease and the torque produced by the small mass will increase.

5. A: When the rope is not parallel to the intended path of motion, the force is divided into useful force (x direction) and not useful force (y direction). If only some of the force is useful, then the man will need to apply more force to achieve the same pulling force as if the rope were parallel to the table.

6. B: Because the volume of the liquid doesn't change, when the small piston is compressed, the volume decrease in one piston is the volume increase in the other piston. As the volume is the area times the height, the height of the larger piston only needs to raise one fourth the height that the small piston moved.

7. A: The downward force decreases part of the y component of the top force, but does not affect the x component of the force. Thus, the resultant force is up and to the right.

8. B: because the same volume of water has to flow through all parts of the river, the water will slow down to fill the wide section.

9. C: The negative side of magnet 2 will be attracted to the positive side of magnet 1. The positive side of magnet 2 will be attracted to the negative side of magnet 3 with the same force. Because the magnitudes of the forces are equal and the directions are opposite, the sum of the forces will be zero.

10. C: The first phase change is from solid to liquid at -21°C. The next phase change is from liquid to gas at 81°C. 90°C is only slightly higher than 81°C, making it safe to say that the substance is still a gas.

11. A: Substitute token values for the resistors to solve. Using 1 Ω resistors, the resistance of circuit A, having resistors in series, is the simple sum of the two resistors: 2 Ω. Because the resistors in circuit B are in parallel, the resistance of circuit B is the reciprocal of the sum of the reciprocals of the resistances, or $\frac{1}{\frac{1}{1}+\frac{1}{1}}$. the result is 1/2 Ω.

12. A: To find the number of swings in a time period from the frequency, multiply the frequency times the time period, after converting the time period into seconds to match the frequency. The final calculation is $\frac{1.4\ swings}{second} * 1\ minute * \frac{60\ seconds}{1\ minute} = 84\ swings$

13. B: The mechanical advantage is calculated by the output force divided by the input force. Because both pistons are the same size, the output force will equal the input force, resulting in a mechanical advantage of one.

14. C: Because the horizontal component of the thrown ball's velocity will not affect the vertical component, the vertical component of the thrown ball's velocity will be identical to the dropped ball's velocity. The balls will hit at the same time.

15. A: The cam has four bumps on it. The needle will move up and down for each bump. The cam will rotate five times in the time period of one minute. The total times the needle will move up and down will be five times four.

16. C: Torque is the product of a force perpendicular to the arm and the length of the arm. Options A and B each increase one part of the torque calculation. However, angling the force towards the center would decrease the part of the force that is acting perpendicular to the arm, as some of the force will be acting inward.

17. B: When the ball is compressed into the spring, the ball has potential stored in the spring. When the ball is flying upwards, the ball has kinetic energy associated with the motion.

18. B: Pressure increases with depth in water. When the tank was lower it experienced more pressure. Thus, when the tank is higher it experiences less pressure.

19. B: Specific gravity can be calculated as the ratio of the density of the liquid in question to the density of water. Because salt water has a higher density than water, the ratio will be greater than one.

20. B: Convective heat transfer deals with the transfer of heat by fluids (including gas). Steam is a fluid which transfers heat to objects, like a hand, with lower temperatures than it.

21. C: A capacitor stores voltage across a gap between two conductive materials.

22. A: Torque is the product of a force perpendicular to the arm and the length of the arm. Wrench A, with the longer arm, will be able to achieve greater amounts of torque with a set force.

23. B: Because the circuit only has one path and the two resistors are in series, the current is the same everywhere in the circuit. The voltage will drop over both resistors. Also, because the circuit is complete, there is current in the circuit.

24. C: Ammeters measure current (think amps). Multimeters measure current and voltage. Voltmeters only measure voltage.

25. B: When the ball is flying upwards, the kinetic energy is being converted into potential energy. Potential energy increases linearly with height, meaning that an object at 2 feet over the ground has twice the potential energy of the object at 1 foot over the ground. Thus, if all of the energy of the ball will be converted from kinetic energy, and half of the energy will be converted at half the height, the potential energy of the ball will be 50 ft-lb.

26. A: Because mechanical advantage is the ratio of output force to input force, an increase in mechanical advantage means, in this case, that the output force will be increasing. However, energy in simple machines is conserved. This means that the work, or force times distance, done to the input will need to increase, while keeping the force the same. Increasing the distance of the applied force will increase the work, allowing for an increased force for the output.

27. A: As the drum spins one full turn, the hanging rope increases length by 1 foot and decreases length by 3.5 feet. Thus, every spin decreases the rope length by 2.5 feet. In two turns, the rope will decrease length by 5 feet. The pulley makes the weight lift half the distance that the rope decreased. Thus, the weight raises 2.5 feet.

28. C: Condensation from the air occurs when the water vapor in the air cools down enough to change phase from vapor to liquid water. If a pipe is cold and the air is warm, the water vapor will condense on the pipe.

29. A: The color, black, will absorb the most heat from radiation.

30. B: The gear ratio between the small and large gears is 18/30 or 3/5. Multiply the number of rotations of the small gear times the gear ratio to get (3 rotations)*(3/5) = 1.8 rotations.

Aviation and Nautical Information Test

1. B: The name of a runway pointing due east would be Runway 9. The names of runways are based on the compass. A runway pointing due south would be Runway 18, and a runway pointing due west would be Runway 27. Of course, every runway will be called by two names, depending on which direction planes are traveling on it. Runway 9 will become Runway 27 when the planes travel west rather than east. When the names of runways are spoken, each number in the name is stated individually. So, Runway 24 would be spoken, "Runway Two-Four" rather than "Runway Twenty-four."

2. E: The powerplant supplies the thrust for a fixed-wing aircraft. The powerplant may be a jet engine or an engine and a set of propellers. Thrust is the force that propels the plane forward.

3. A: The chord line runs through the wing from the leading edge to the trailing edge. This line divides the upper and lower surfaces of the wing. This is one of the key elements of wing design. The distance from one wingtip to the other, meanwhile, is called the wingspan. The mean camber line runs along the inside of the wing, such that the upper and lower wings are equal in thickness.

4. E: A plane will tend to remain in a medium bank until the pilot makes an adjustment. A medium bank is between 20 and 45 degrees. A shallow bank, on the other hand, is less than 20 degrees, and requires the assistance of the ailerons to maintain itself. A steep bank is greater than 45 degrees. When a plane enters a steep bank, it will tend to increase the bank unless the ailerons are used to prevent this. Turning occurs because of the forces that act on a banked wing. The plane will be pushed in a direction perpendicular to the wings.

5. B: Spin is not one of the four basic maneuvers in flight. Straight-and-level flight, turns, climbs, and descents are the four basic flight maneuvers. Straight-and-level flight occurs when the plane maintains a constant altitude and is pointed in the same direction. Of course, maintaining the same altitude and direction requires a number of adjustments. Turns are made by banking the wings in the direction of the turn: that is, for example, turning to the right requires lowering the right wing. A climb requires raising the nose of the plane and increasing the power from the engine. Finally, there are a few types of descent. A plane may descend with its nose up, down, or level.

6. E: The angled flight deck was the main innovation that allowed widespread use of jets on aircraft carriers. Due to their high speeds, jet landings on aircraft carriers were extremely dangerous. If the aircraft missed all the arrestor cables, the jet would crash into the parked planes on the carrier. With an angled flight deck, if the jet misses all the arrestor cables, the pilot can hit maximum speed and be launched into the air, missing the parked aircraft.

7. C: A Visual Approach Slope Indicator should be visible from approximately twenty miles away at night. A Visual Approach Slope Indicator (VASI) is a common feature at large airports. This system helps guide the approaching pilot to the runway. The pilot will see white lights at the lower border of the glide path, and red lights at the upper border. In normal conditions, the lights of the VASI system should be visible for three to five miles during the day, and for twenty miles at night. If the VASI system is working properly, the plane will be safe so long as it stays within ten degrees of the extended runway centerline and four nautical miles of the runway threshold.

8. E: Torque is not one of the forces a pilot must manage during flight. The four forces a pilot must manage are lift, gravity, thrust, and drag. Lift pushes the plane up, gravity pulls the plane down, thrust propels the plane forward, and drag holds the plane back. The overall admixture of these forces as they operate on the plane is called the flight envelope.

9. A: The collective affects the angle of the main rotor blades of a helicopter. It is a long tube that extends from the floor of the cockpit. In most helicopters, it is situated on the pilot's left. The collective has two parts: a handle that can be raised or lowered, to control the pitch of the blades; and a throttle, to control the torque of the engine. The handle is the part that affects the angle of the main rotor blades. When it is raised, the leading edge of the blade is raised higher than the trailing edge.

10. D: Edwin Dunning, an officer in the British Royal Navy Air Service, was the first person in history to land an aircraft on a moving ship. Others had landed planes on docked ships, but never on one at sea. Commander Dunning landed a Sopwith Pup on the HMS *Furious* on August 2nd, 1917. Tragically, he drowned five days later, when his plane was caught in an upwind and thrown overboard while he was attempting to perform another landing.

11. C: The flight attitude is the position of a plane in motion. The flight attitude is described in terms of its position with respect to three axes: vertical, lateral, and longitudinal. The vertical axis runs up through the plane's center of gravity. A plane's position with respect to this axis is known as its yaw. The lateral axis of a plane runs from wingtip to wingtip, and the motion of the plane around this axis is known as pitch. The longitudinal axis, finally, is an imaginary line extending from the nose of the plane to its tail. The position of the plane in relation to the longitudinal axis is called roll. The attitude of the plane is controlled with the joystick, rudder pedals, and throttle.

12. C: The curvature of an airfoil is known as the camber. An airfoil (wing) is considered to have a high camber if it is very curved. A related piece of wing terminology is the mean camber line, which runs along the inside of the wing, such that the upper and lower wings are equal in thickness.

13. A: The elevators are considered one of the primary flight controls. The elevators are responsible for the plane's pitch, or movement around the lateral axis. The other primary flight controls are the ailerons and the rudder. The ailerons control the roll, or movement around the longitudinal axis, while the rudder controls the yaw, or movement around the vertical axis. The secondary flight controls are the flaps, spoilers, leading edge devices, and trim systems.

14. B: In aviation, the term for movement around the plane's longitudinal axis is rolling. The longitudinal axis runs from the nose of the plane to its tail. For the most part, the plane's roll is controlled by the joystick. By moving the stick to the right or left, the pilot dips the wings.

15. D: Power-up. Optical landing systems feature wave-off, ball, ("meatball"), datum, and cut lights, but they do not employ power-up lights.

16. A: Japan created the world's first purpose-built aircraft carrier in 1921, the Hōshō. Other ships in various countries had been converted into aircraft carriers, but the Hōshō was the first ship in the world built deliberately as an aircraft carrier. England had begun work on their own purpose-built aircraft carrier (HMS *Hermes*) earlier, but Japan completed theirs first.

17. D: The vertical axis of a plane extends up through the plane's center of gravity. Movement around this axis is called yawing. The position of a plane is also described with respect to the lateral and longitudinal axes. The lateral axis extends from wingtip to wingtip. The longitudinal axis runs from the nose of the plane to its tail.

18. E: Trimming is necessary after any change in the flight condition. Trimming is the adjustment of the trim tabs, which are small flaps that extend from the trailing edges of the elevators, rudder, and ailerons. Trimming generally occurs after the pilot has achieved the desired pitch, power, attitude, and configuration. The trim tabs are then used to resolve the remaining control pressures. A small plane may only have a single tab, which is controlled with a small wheel or crank.

157

19. B: When the Runway Centerline Lighting System lights become solid red, an approaching plane is one thousand feet away. A Runway Centerline Lighting System is a line of white lights every fifty feet or so along the centerline. The lights change their color and pattern as the plane nears the runway. When the plane gets within 3000 feet of the runway, the lights blink red and white. Within a thousand feet, the lights will turn solid red.

20. E: The Coriolis force is the change in rotational speed caused by the shift of the weight towards or away from the center of the spinning object. This phenomenon has an important application for helicopters, in which the rotor will move faster or will require less power to maintain its speed when the weight is closer to the base of the blade. The other answer choices are similarly related to helicopters. The extra lift generated by a helicopter once it has exited its own downwash is known as translational lift. The force that spins the rotors of a helicopter even when there is no power from the engine is autorotation. Greater downwash at the rear half of the rotor disc, as compared to the front half, is the result of applying the lateral cyclic. The phenomenon in which the effects of a force applied to a spinning disc occur ninety degrees later is called gyroscopic precession.

21. A: The altitude at which the plane is flying is the primary determinant of air pressure in the flight envelope. The most important elements of the flight envelope are the temperature, air pressure, and humidity. The conditions in the atmosphere have a great deal of influence over the amount of lift created by the airfoils. Greater air pressure is the same as greater air density. A plane will generate greater lift when it is in cool air, because cool air is less dense than warm air.

22. B: A plane is said to have conventional landing gear when the third wheel is under the tail. Typically, a plane's landing gear will consist of three wheels or sets of wheels. Two of these are under either wing or on opposing sides of the fuselage. In the conventional arrangement, the third wheel or wheel set is under the tail, while in the tricycle arrangement it is under the nose. This third wheel can rotate, which will make it possible for the plane to turn while moving on the ground.

23. B: The USS *Enterprise* was America's first nuclear-powered aircraft carrier. It was launched on September 24th, 1960, commissioned on November 25th, 1961, and it embarked on its maiden voyage on January 12th, 1962.

24. B: Charles Samson was the first person in history to fly an aircraft from a moving ship. Others before him had taken off from docked ships, but never a ship at sea. He took off from the HMS *Hibernia* on May 9, 1912.

25. D: An aileron is not part of the empennage. The empennage, otherwise known as the tail assembly, includes the elevators, vertical and horizontal stabilizers, rudders, and trim tabs. A fixed wing aircraft will typically have both vertical and horizontal stabilizers, which are immobile surfaces that extend from the back of the fuselage. The horizontal stabilizers have mobile surfaces along their trailing edges; these surfaces are called the elevators. The elevators deflect up and down to raise or lower the nose of the plane. The rudder is a single, large flap connected by a hinge to the vertical stabilizer. The rudders back-and-forth motion controls the motion of the plane with respect to its vertical axis. The trim tabs, finally, are connected to the trailing edges of one or more of the primary flight controls (i.e., ailerons, elevators, rudder).

26. E: A glider would be most likely to have a straight wing. A straight wing may be tapered, elliptical, or rectangular. This planform (wing shape) is common in aircraft that move at extremely low speed. A straight wing is often found on sailplanes and gliders. The swept wing, on the other hand, is appropriate for high-speed aircraft. The wing may be swept forward or back. This will make the plane unstable at low speeds, but will produce much less drag. A swept wing requires high-speed takeoff and landing. The delta wing, which is also known as the triangular wing, has a straight trailing edge and a high angle of sweep. This allows the plane to take off and land at high speeds.

27. A: The crew is not considered part of a plane's basic weight. The basic weight is the aircraft plus whatever internal or external equipment will remain on the plane during its journey. The crew is not included in the basic weight, though it is a part of the operating weight (basic weight plus crew), gross weight (total weight of the aircraft at any particular time), landing gross weight (weight of the plane and its contents upon touchdown), and zero fuel weight (weight of the airplane when it has no usable fuel).

28. D: The support structure that runs the length of the fuselage in a monocoque plane is called a stringer. In a monocoque plane, the fuselage is supported by stringers, formers, and bulkheads. Stringers and formers are generally made out of the same material, though they run perpendicular to one another (that is, formers run in circles around the width of the fuselage). Bulkheads are the walls that divide the sections of the fuselage. The other style of fuselage, known as a truss, is composed of triangular groupings of aluminum or steel tubing.

29. C: The joystick is used to manipulate the elevators. When the stick is pulled back, the elevators deflect upwards. This decreases the camber of the horizontal tail surface, which moves the nose up and pushes the tail down. Pushing the joystick forward, on the other hand, pushes the elevators down, which creates an upward force on the tail by increasing the camber of the horizontal tail surface.

30. A: When a pilot needs to descend quickly onto a shorter-than-normal runway, he or she will descend at the minimum safe airspeed. A descent at the minimum safe airspeed is achieved by slightly lifting the nose and moving the plane into the landing configuration. During such a descent, the plane should not exceed 1.3 times the stall speed. This technique is appropriate for landing quickly on a short runway because the rate of descent is much faster. However, if the rate of descent should become too great, the pilot should be ready to increase power.

Bonus Section: Spatial Apperception

While there is no Spatial Apperception subtest on the ASTB-E, practicing spatial apperception skills can help you perform better on the Performance Based Measures Battery. These types of problems are based on visual information rather than written text or mathematical problems. The word *apperception* refers to the process by which you interpret some new information using the knowledge you already possess.

These questions are measuring your ability to translate visual information from one perspective into an accurate mental representation of the same information from a completely different perspective. Military test developers have determined that this ability is critical to success in flight school and as a pilot, and they have also determined that the Spatial Apperception test is very accurate at measuring a person's aptitude and abilities in this area.

For each question, you'll first be shown a drawing of a terrain with a horizon, from the point of view of a pilot in the cockpit of an aircraft above the terrain. Then you'll be shown five more drawings of the aircraft from the perspective of someone on the ground observing the craft, each showing the aircraft in a different attitude. You will be required to determine which of the five drawings shows the aircraft in the attitude that would provide the view of the terrain shown in the first illustration to someone looking straight out of the cockpit of the aircraft.

The most important thing to keep in mind is that you're really only looking for three pieces of information. The three questions you'll need to answer for each drawing are:

- What is the vertical orientation of the aircraft? Is it climbing, diving, or flying straight ahead?
- Are the wings level, is the aircraft banking left, or is it banking right?
- In which direction is the aircraft heading?

Practice Questions

Instructions: The view shown on each question is a view from the cockpit of an aircraft in flight. Select the answer letter that best represents the orientation of the aircraft as seen from the ground.

1.

a.   b.   c.   d.   e.

2.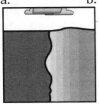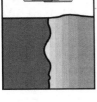

a.   b.   c.   d.   e.

3.

a.   b.   c.   d.   e.

4.

a.   b.   c.   d.   e.

5.

a.   b.   c.   d.   e.

6.

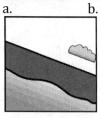

a.   b.   c.   d.   e.

7.

a.   b.   c.   d.   e.

8.

a.   b.   c.   d.   e.

9.

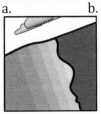

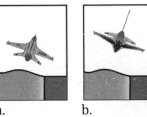 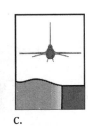 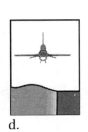 

a.   b.   c.   d.   e.

10.

a.   b.   c.   d.   e.

11.

      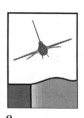

a.   b.   c.   d.   e.

12.

a.   b.   c.   d.   e.

13.

 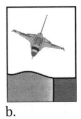   

a.   b.   c.   d.   e.

14.

 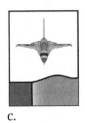  

a.   b.   c.   d.   e.

15.

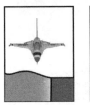    

a.   b.   c.   d.   e.

16.

 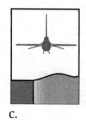  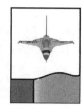

a.   b.   c.   d.   e.

17.

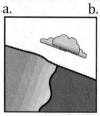

a.   b.   c.   d.   e.

18.

a.   b.   c.   d.   e.

19.

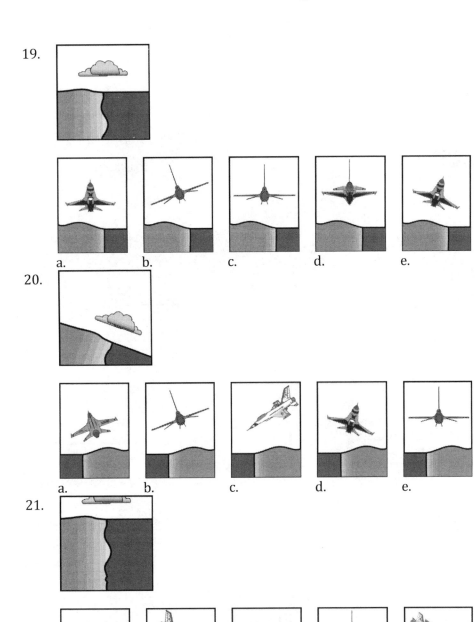

a.

b.

c.

d.

e.

20.

a.

b.

c.

d.

e.

21.

a.

b.

c.

d.

e.

22.

a.   b.   c.   d.   e.

23.

  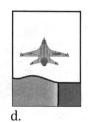 

a.   b.   c.   d.   e.

24.

a.   b.   c.   d.   e.

25.

a.   b.   c.   d.   e.

169

Answer Key

Problem	Answer	Description
1	B	out to sea, diving, and banking right
2	D	coastline right, diving, and wings level
3	E	coastline right, level flight, and banking left
4	B	coastline right, diving, and banking right
5	E	coastline left, climbing, and wings level
6	D	out to sea, level flight, and banking left
7	A	out to sea, diving, and banking left
8	A	out to sea, climbing, and wings level
9	B	coastline left, diving, and banking right
10	B	coastline left, level flight, and banking right
11	B	coastline right, climbing, and wings level
12	D	out to sea, climbing, and banking left
13	C	coastline left, diving, and banking left
14	B	coastline left, climbing, and banking right
15	C	coastline right, level flight, and banking right
16	C	coastline right, level flight, and wings level
17	B	coastline left, level flight, and banking left
18	B	coastline left, climbing, and banking right
19	C	coastline left, level flight, and wings level
20	D	coastline left, climbing, and banking left
21	D	coastline left, diving, and wings level
22	C	coastline right, climbing, and banking right
23	A	out to sea, level flight, and wings level
24	D	out to sea, diving, and wings level
25	B	out to sea, level flight, and banking right

How to Overcome Test Anxiety

Just the thought of taking a test is enough to make most people a little nervous. A test is an important event that can have a long-term impact on your future, so it's important to take it seriously and it's natural to feel anxious about performing well. But just because anxiety is normal, that doesn't mean that it's helpful in test taking, or that you should simply accept it as part of your life. Anxiety can have a variety of effects. These effects can be mild, like making you feel slightly nervous, or severe, like blocking your ability to focus or remember even a simple detail.

If you experience test anxiety—whether severe or mild—it's important to know how to beat it. To discover this, first you need to understand what causes test anxiety.

Causes of Test Anxiety

While we often think of anxiety as an uncontrollable emotional state, it can actually be caused by simple, practical things. One of the most common causes of test anxiety is that a person does not feel adequately prepared for their test. This feeling can be the result of many different issues such as poor study habits or lack of organization, but the most common culprit is time management. Starting to study too late, failing to organize your study time to cover all of the material, or being distracted while you study will mean that you're not well prepared for the test. This may lead to cramming the night before, which will cause you to be physically and mentally exhausted for the test. Poor time management also contributes to feelings of stress, fear, and hopelessness as you realize you are not well prepared but don't know what to do about it.

Other times, test anxiety is not related to your preparation for the test but comes from unresolved fear. This may be a past failure on a test, or poor performance on tests in general. It may come from comparing yourself to others who seem to be performing better or from the stress of living up to expectations. Anxiety may be driven by fears of the future—how failure on this test would affect your educational and career goals. These fears are often completely irrational, but they can still negatively impact your test performance.

Review Video: <u>3 Reasons You Have Test Anxiety</u>
Visit mometrix.com/academy and enter code: 428468

Elements of Test Anxiety

As mentioned earlier, test anxiety is considered to be an emotional state, but it has physical and mental components as well. Sometimes you may not even realize that you are suffering from test anxiety until you notice the physical symptoms. These can include trembling hands, rapid heartbeat, sweating, nausea, and tense muscles. Extreme anxiety may lead to fainting or vomiting. Obviously, any of these symptoms can have a negative impact on testing. It is important to recognize them as soon as they begin to occur so that you can address the problem before it damages your performance.

> **Review Video: 3 Ways to Tell You Have Test Anxiety**
> Visit mometrix.com/academy and enter code: 927847

The mental components of test anxiety include trouble focusing and inability to remember learned information. During a test, your mind is on high alert, which can help you recall information and stay focused for an extended period of time. However, anxiety interferes with your mind's natural processes, causing you to blank out, even on the questions you know well. The strain of testing during anxiety makes it difficult to stay focused, especially on a test that may take several hours. Extreme anxiety can take a huge mental toll, making it difficult not only to recall test information but even to understand the test questions or pull your thoughts together.

> **Review Video: How Test Anxiety Affects Memory**
> Visit mometrix.com/academy and enter code: 609003

Effects of Test Anxiety

Test anxiety is like a disease—if left untreated, it will get progressively worse. Anxiety leads to poor performance, and this reinforces the feelings of fear and failure, which in turn lead to poor performances on subsequent tests. It can grow from a mild nervousness to a crippling condition. If allowed to progress, test anxiety can have a big impact on your schooling, and consequently on your future.

Test anxiety can spread to other parts of your life. Anxiety on tests can become anxiety in any stressful situation, and blanking on a test can turn into panicking in a job situation. But fortunately, you don't have to let anxiety rule your testing and determine your grades. There are a number of relatively simple steps you can take to move past anxiety and function normally on a test and in the rest of life.

> **Review Video: How Test Anxiety Impacts Your Grades**
> Visit mometrix.com/academy and enter code: 939819

Physical Steps for Beating Test Anxiety

While test anxiety is a serious problem, the good news is that it can be overcome. It doesn't have to control your ability to think and remember information. While it may take time, you can begin taking steps today to beat anxiety.

Just as your first hint that you may be struggling with anxiety comes from the physical symptoms, the first step to treating it is also physical. Rest is crucial for having a clear, strong mind. If you are tired, it is much easier to give in to anxiety. But if you establish good sleep habits, your body and mind will be ready to perform optimally, without the strain of exhaustion. Additionally, sleeping well helps you to retain information better, so you're more likely to recall the answers when you see the test questions.

Getting good sleep means more than going to bed on time. It's important to allow your brain time to relax. Take study breaks from time to time so it doesn't get overworked, and don't study right before bed. Take time to rest your mind before trying to rest your body, or you may find it difficult to fall asleep.

Review Video: The Importance of Sleep for Your Brain
Visit mometrix.com/academy and enter code: 319338

Along with sleep, other aspects of physical health are important in preparing for a test. Good nutrition is vital for good brain function. Sugary foods and drinks may give a burst of energy but this burst is followed by a crash, both physically and emotionally. Instead, fuel your body with protein and vitamin-rich foods.

Also, drink plenty of water. Dehydration can lead to headaches and exhaustion, especially if your brain is already under stress from the rigors of the test. Particularly if your test is a long one, drink water during the breaks. And if possible, take an energy-boosting snack to eat between sections.

Review Video: How Diet Can Affect your Mood
Visit mometrix.com/academy and enter code: 624317

Along with sleep and diet, a third important part of physical health is exercise. Maintaining a steady workout schedule is helpful, but even taking 5-minute study breaks to walk can help get your blood pumping faster and clear your head. Exercise also releases endorphins, which contribute to a positive feeling and can help combat test anxiety.

When you nurture your physical health, you are also contributing to your mental health. If your body is healthy, your mind is much more likely to be healthy as well. So take time to rest, nourish your body with healthy food and water, and get moving as much as possible. Taking these physical steps will make you stronger and more able to take the mental steps necessary to overcome test anxiety.

Review Video: How to Stay Healthy and Prevent Test Anxiety
Visit mometrix.com/academy and enter code: 877894

Mental Steps for Beating Test Anxiety

Working on the mental side of test anxiety can be more challenging, but as with the physical side, there are clear steps you can take to overcome it. As mentioned earlier, test anxiety often stems from lack of preparation, so the obvious solution is to prepare for the test. Effective studying may be the most important weapon you have for beating test anxiety, but you can and should employ several other mental tools to combat fear.

First, boost your confidence by reminding yourself of past success—tests or projects that you aced. If you're putting as much effort into preparing for this test as you did for those, there's no reason you should expect to fail here. Work hard to prepare; then trust your preparation.

Second, surround yourself with encouraging people. It can be helpful to find a study group, but be sure that the people you're around will encourage a positive attitude. If you spend time with others who are anxious or cynical, this will only contribute to your own anxiety. Look for others who are motivated to study hard from a desire to succeed, not from a fear of failure.

Third, reward yourself. A test is physically and mentally tiring, even without anxiety, and it can be helpful to have something to look forward to. Plan an activity following the test, regardless of the outcome, such as going to a movie or getting ice cream.

When you are taking the test, if you find yourself beginning to feel anxious, remind yourself that you know the material. Visualize successfully completing the test. Then take a few deep, relaxing breaths and return to it. Work through the questions carefully but with confidence, knowing that you are capable of succeeding.

Developing a healthy mental approach to test taking will also aid in other areas of life. Test anxiety affects more than just the actual test—it can be damaging to your mental health and even contribute to depression. It's important to beat test anxiety before it becomes a problem for more than testing.

Review Video: <u>Test Anxiety and Depression</u>
Visit mometrix.com/academy and enter code: 904704

Study Strategy

Being prepared for the test is necessary to combat anxiety, but what does being prepared look like? You may study for hours on end and still not feel prepared. What you need is a strategy for test prep. The next few pages outline our recommended steps to help you plan out and conquer the challenge of preparation.

STEP 1: SCOPE OUT THE TEST

Learn everything you can about the format (multiple choice, essay, etc.) and what will be on the test. Gather any study materials, course outlines, or sample exams that may be available. Not only will this help you to prepare, but knowing what to expect can help to alleviate test anxiety.

STEP 2: MAP OUT THE MATERIAL

Look through the textbook or study guide and make note of how many chapters or sections it has. Then divide these over the time you have. For example, if a book has 15 chapters and you have five days to study, you need to cover three chapters each day. Even better, if you have the time, leave an extra day at the end for overall review after you have gone through the material in depth.

If time is limited, you may need to prioritize the material. Look through it and make note of which sections you think you already have a good grasp on, and which need review. While you are studying, skim quickly through the familiar sections and take more time on the challenging parts. Write out your plan so you don't get lost as you go. Having a written plan also helps you feel more in control of the study, so anxiety is less likely to arise from feeling overwhelmed at the amount to cover.

STEP 3: GATHER YOUR TOOLS

Decide what study method works best for you. Do you prefer to highlight in the book as you study and then go back over the highlighted portions? Or do you type out notes of the important information? Or is it helpful to make flashcards that you can carry with you? Assemble the pens, index cards, highlighters, post-it notes, and any other materials you may need so you won't be distracted by getting up to find things while you study.

If you're having a hard time retaining the information or organizing your notes, experiment with different methods. For example, try color-coding by subject with colored pens, highlighters, or post-it notes. If you learn better by hearing, try recording yourself reading your notes so you can listen while in the car, working out, or simply sitting at your desk. Ask a friend to quiz you from your flashcards, or try teaching someone the material to solidify it in your mind.

STEP 4: CREATE YOUR ENVIRONMENT

It's important to avoid distractions while you study. This includes both the obvious distractions like visitors and the subtle distractions like an uncomfortable chair (or a too-comfortable couch that makes you want to fall asleep). Set up the best study environment possible: good lighting and a comfortable work area. If background music helps you focus, you may want to turn it on, but otherwise keep the room quiet. If you are using a computer to take notes, be sure you don't have any other windows open, especially applications like social media, games, or anything else that could distract you. Silence your phone and turn off notifications. Be sure to keep water close by so you stay hydrated while you study (but avoid unhealthy drinks and snacks).

Also, take into account the best time of day to study. Are you freshest first thing in the morning? Try to set aside some time then to work through the material. Is your mind clearer in the afternoon or evening? Schedule your study session then. Another method is to study at the same time of day that you will take the test, so that your brain gets used to working on the material at that time and will be ready to focus at test time.

STEP 5: STUDY!

Once you have done all the study preparation, it's time to settle into the actual studying. Sit down, take a few moments to settle your mind so you can focus, and begin to follow your study plan. Don't give in to distractions or let yourself procrastinate. This is your time to prepare so you'll be ready to fearlessly approach the test. Make the most of the time and stay focused.

Of course, you don't want to burn out. If you study too long you may find that you're not retaining the information very well. Take regular study breaks. For example, taking five minutes out of every hour to walk briskly, breathing deeply and swinging your arms, can help your mind stay fresh.

As you get to the end of each chapter or section, it's a good idea to do a quick review. Remind yourself of what you learned and work on any difficult parts. When you feel that you've mastered the material, move on to the next part. At the end of your study session, briefly skim through your notes again.

But while review is helpful, cramming last minute is NOT. If at all possible, work ahead so that you won't need to fit all your study into the last day. Cramming overloads your brain with more information than it can process and retain, and your tired mind may struggle to recall even previously learned information when it is overwhelmed with last-minute study. Also, the urgent nature of cramming and the stress placed on your brain contribute to anxiety. You'll be more likely to go to the test feeling unprepared and having trouble thinking clearly.

So don't cram, and don't stay up late before the test, even just to review your notes at a leisurely pace. Your brain needs rest more than it needs to go over the information again. In fact, plan to finish your studies by noon or early afternoon the day before the test. Give your brain the rest of the day to relax or focus on other things, and get a good night's sleep. Then you will be fresh for the test and better able to recall what you've studied.

STEP 6: TAKE A PRACTICE TEST

Many courses offer sample tests, either online or in the study materials. This is an excellent resource to check whether you have mastered the material, as well as to prepare for the test format and environment.

Check the test format ahead of time: the number of questions, the type (multiple choice, free response, etc.), and the time limit. Then create a plan for working through them. For example, if you have 30 minutes to take a 60-question test, your limit is 30 seconds per question. Spend less time on the questions you know well so that you can take more time on the difficult ones.

If you have time to take several practice tests, take the first one open book, with no time limit. Work through the questions at your own pace and make sure you fully understand them. Gradually work up to taking a test under test conditions: sit at a desk with all study materials put away and set a timer. Pace yourself to make sure you finish the test with time to spare and go back to check your answers if you have time.

After each test, check your answers. On the questions you missed, be sure you understand why you missed them. Did you misread the question (tests can use tricky wording)? Did you forget the information? Or was it something you hadn't learned? Go back and study any shaky areas that the practice tests reveal.

Taking these tests not only helps with your grade, but also aids in combating test anxiety. If you're already used to the test conditions, you're less likely to worry about it, and working through tests until you're scoring well gives you a confidence boost. Go through the practice tests until you feel comfortable, and then you can go into the test knowing that you're ready for it.

Test Tips

On test day, you should be confident, knowing that you've prepared well and are ready to answer the questions. But aside from preparation, there are several test day strategies you can employ to maximize your performance.

First, as stated before, get a good night's sleep the night before the test (and for several nights before that, if possible). Go into the test with a fresh, alert mind rather than staying up late to study.

Try not to change too much about your normal routine on the day of the test. It's important to eat a nutritious breakfast, but if you normally don't eat breakfast at all, consider eating just a protein bar. If you're a coffee drinker, go ahead and have your normal coffee. Just make sure you time it so that the caffeine doesn't wear off right in the middle of your test. Avoid sugary beverages, and drink enough water to stay hydrated but not so much that you need a restroom break 10 minutes into the test. If your test isn't first thing in the morning, consider going for a walk or doing a light workout before the test to get your blood flowing.

Allow yourself enough time to get ready, and leave for the test with plenty of time to spare so you won't have the anxiety of scrambling to arrive in time. Another reason to be early is to select a good seat. It's helpful to sit away from doors and windows, which can be distracting. Find a good seat, get out your supplies, and settle your mind before the test begins.

When the test begins, start by going over the instructions carefully, even if you already know what to expect. Make sure you avoid any careless mistakes by following the directions.

Then begin working through the questions, pacing yourself as you've practiced. If you're not sure on an answer, don't spend too much time on it, and don't let it shake your confidence. Either skip it and come back later, or eliminate as many wrong answers as possible and guess among the remaining ones. Don't dwell on these questions as you continue—put them out of your mind and focus on what lies ahead.

Be sure to read all of the answer choices, even if you're sure the first one is the right answer. Sometimes you'll find a better one if you keep reading. But don't second-guess yourself if you do immediately know the answer. Your gut instinct is usually right. Don't let test anxiety rob you of the information you know.

If you have time at the end of the test (and if the test format allows), go back and review your answers. Be cautious about changing any, since your first instinct tends to be correct, but make sure you didn't misread any of the questions or accidentally mark the wrong answer choice. Look over any you skipped and make an educated guess.

At the end, leave the test feeling confident. You've done your best, so don't waste time worrying about your performance or wishing you could change anything. Instead, celebrate the successful completion of this test. And finally, use this test to learn how to deal with anxiety even better next time.

Review Video: 5 Tips to Beat Test Anxiety
Visit mometrix.com/academy and enter code: 570656

Important Qualification

Not all anxiety is created equal. If your test anxiety is causing major issues in your life beyond the classroom or testing center, or if you are experiencing troubling physical symptoms related to your anxiety, it may be a sign of a serious physiological or psychological condition. If this sounds like your situation, we strongly encourage you to seek professional help.

Thank You

We at Mometrix would like to extend our heartfelt thanks to you, our friend and patron, for allowing us to play a part in your journey. It is a privilege to serve people from all walks of life who are unified in their commitment to building the best future they can for themselves.

The preparation you devote to these important testing milestones may be the most valuable educational opportunity you have for making a real difference in your life. We encourage you to put your heart into it—that feeling of succeeding, overcoming, and yes, conquering will be well worth the hours you've invested.

We want to hear your story, your struggles and your successes, and if you see any opportunities for us to improve our materials so we can help others even more effectively in the future, please share that with us as well. **The team at Mometrix would be absolutely thrilled to hear from you!** So please, send us an email (support@mometrix.com) and let's stay in touch.

Additional Bonus Material

Due to our efforts to try to keep this book to a manageable length, we've created a link that will give you access to all of your additional bonus material.

Please visit https://www.mometrix.com/bonus948/astbe to access the information.